# THINKING OF OTHERS

PRINCETON MONOGRAPHS

IN PHILOSOPHY

*Harry G. Frankfurt, Editor*

—————————— ¶MP ——————————

The Princeton Monographs in Philosophy series offers short

historical and systematic studies on a wide variety

of philosophical topics.

*Justice Is Conflict* by STUART HAMPSHIRE

*Liberty Worth the Name: Locke on Free Agency* by GIDEON YAFFE

*Self-Deception Unmasked* by ALFRED R. MELE

*Public Goods, Private Goods* by RAYMOND GEUSS

*Welfare and Rational Care* by STEPHEN DARWALL

*A Defense of Hume on Miracles* by ROBERT J. FOGELIN

*Kierkegaard's Concept of Despair* by MICHAEL THEUNISSEN
(TRANSLATED BY BARBARA HARSHAV AND HELMUT ILLBRUCK)

*Physicalism, or Something Near Enough* by JAEGWON KIM

*Philosophical Myths of the Fall* by STEPHEN MULHALL

*Fixing Frege* by JOHN P. BURGESS

*Kant and Skepticism* by MICHAEL N. FORSTER

*Thinking of Others: On the Talent for Metaphor*
by TED COHEN

# THINKING OF
# OTHERS

## ON THE TALENT FOR METAPHOR

*Ted Cohen*

PRINCETON UNIVERSITY PRESS

PRINCETON AND OXFORD

Copyright © 2008 by Princeton University Press
Published by Princeton University Press, 41 William Street,
Princeton, New Jersey 08540
In the United Kingdom: Princeton University Press, 6 Oxford Street,
Woodstock, Oxfordshire OX20 1TW

All Rights Reserved

Library of Congress Cataloging-in-Publication Data

Cohen, Ted.
Thinking of others : on the talent for metaphor / Ted Cohen.
    p.   cm. — (Princeton monographs in philosophy)
Includes index.
ISBN 978-0-691-13746-9 (cloth : alk. paper)
    1. Metaphor. 2. Empathy. I. Title.
PN228.M4C58 2008
808—dc22        2008014920

British Library Cataloging-in-Publication Data is available

This book has been composed in Janson Typeface

Printed on acid-free paper. ∞

press.princeton.edu

Printed in the United States of America

1   3   5   7   9   10   8   6   4   2

*This book is for Andy Austin Cohen*

---

SHE DOES A BETTER JOB OF THINKING OF OTHER
PEOPLE THAN ANYONE ELSE I KNOW, DOING IT WITH
UNDERSTANDING AND GENEROSITY BUT WITHOUT
EVER BEING FOOLISH. LIKE ALL PEOPLE, ANDY IS
UNIQUE; AND SHE IS MORE SO.

# Contents

*Acknowledgments*
ix

CHAPTER ONE
The Talent for Metaphor
1

CHAPTER TWO
Being a Good Sport
13

CHAPTER THREE
From the Bible: Nathan and David
19

CHAPTER FOUR
Real Feelings, Unreal People
29

CHAPTER FIVE
More from the Bible: Abraham and God
53

CHAPTER SIX
More Lessons from Sports
57

CHAPTER SEVEN
Oneself Seen by Others
65

CHAPTER EIGHT
Oneself as Oneself
67

CHAPTER NINE
Lessons from Art
69

CHAPTER TEN
The Possibility of Conversation, Moral and Otherwise
79

CHAPTER ELEVEN
Conclusion: In Praise of Metaphor
85

*Index*
87

# Acknowledgments

SOME OF the material in this book was published in earlier, different versions, under different titles. "Metaphor, Feeling, and Narrative" was published in *Philosophy and Literature*, vol. 21, no. 2 (October, 1997), pp. 223–44. "Identifying with Metaphor: Metaphors of Personal Identification" was delivered as the presidential address to the American Society for Aesthetics in 1998, and subsequently published in the *Journal of Aesthetics and Art Criticism*, vol. 57, no. 4 (Fall, 1999), pp. 399–409. "Stories" was delivered as the presidential address to the Central Division of the American Philosophical Association in 2007, and subsequently published in *Proceedings and Addresses of the American Philosophical Association*, vol. 81, no. 2 (November, 2007), pp. 33–48.

This small text is much better for having been reviewed by three of the best readers I know, Stanley Bates, Stanley Cavell, and David Hills.

Stanley Bates was once my colleague and has been my friend for decades. Except for Howard Stein, I believe Bates reads and knows more than anyone else I know. He showed me that my central idea is connected to more topics, themes, and problems than I had realized.

Stanley Cavell was once my teacher and has been my friend ever since. Years ago I had the privilege of writing and reading out the citation for him when Cavell received an honorary degree, and I hit on what I thought and think a fitting ascription when I said that he has the courage of his affections. It is this model that has made it possible for eccentrics like me to pursue what appeals to us while supposing that we are still philosophers. In the case of this book, it is Cavell who made me understand that I am taken with and speaking of metaphor not in the narrow sense of that word, but in a much more expanded and ambitious sense, a point that has made my project more difficult and more interesting.

David Hills is a rarity, an absolutely first-class analytical philosopher who reads what you write as if he were a master literary reader. I once published a pair of essays together, one autobiographical and the other straightforwardly analytical, leaving completely unexplained how those two pieces might go together. Whatever success those essays enjoyed, I think almost all readers took them to be independent and separable. When I later met Hills he made clear that he had found exactly why they go together. In reading this manuscript, Hills found more than a few lapses, places in which I settled for a nice idea and a pleasant phrase without supplying a foundation that would support them.

It was a pleasure, of course, and also a relief to know that those three thought the material worth sending out. If you do not think so, you might blame them a little, but you should mainly hold me responsible.

# THINKING OF OTHERS

# CHAPTER ONE

## *The Talent for Metaphor*

Nonetheless, I agree that there _is_ a pictorial dimension
to metaphor and that the perspective it generates cannot
be expressed propositionally.
—JOSEF STERN[1]

We may, therefore, regard the metaphorical sentence as a
"Duck-Rabbit"; it is a sentence that may simultaneously be
regarded as presenting two different situations; looked at
one way, it describes the actual situation, and looked at the
other way, an hypothetical situation with which that
situation is being compared.
—ROGER WHITE[2]

THERE is mystery at the heart of metaphor. During the past
several years a number of capable authors have done much to
clarify the topic, and they have shown that some earlier central
theses about the nature of metaphor are untenable.[3] What they

---

[1] *Metaphor in Context* (Cambridge, MA: MIT Press, 2000), p. 289.

[2] *The Structure of Metaphor* (Oxford: Blackwell, 1996), p. 115.

[3] This book makes no effort to contribute to the literature on the topic of
metaphor as such. It aims only to claim that the construction and comprehension of metaphors, however those things may be done, require an ability that
is the same as the human capacity for understanding one another. There are
now two excellent book-length philosophical treatments of metaphor. Anyone
wishing acquaintance with this topic can do no better than starting with them,
and I don't see any other way of doing as well. These texts are not only virtually
definitive of the best current work on the topic, but they are also excellent

have shown, in particular, is that the import of a significant metaphor cannot be delivered literally, that is, in general, that a <u>metaphorical statement has no literal statement that is its equivalent.</u>

It may or may not be prudent to regard the import of a metaphor as a *meaning*. If it is, then a metaphorical sentence has two meanings, one literal and one metaphorical. If not, then there is only one meaning, the literal meaning, and the metaphorical import has to be understood in another way. But in either case there will be a metaphorical import that a competent audience will grasp. How the audience does this is, in the end, a mystery.

In the case of a metaphor of the form '*A* is *B*', some comparison is indicated of the properties of *A* with the properties of *B*. <u>An early idea, persistent at least since Aristotle, is that this comparison can be made explicit in a formulation of the form '*A* is like *B*' and this leads to the further idea that the import of the metaphor can be expressed as an explicit, literal comparison of *A* with *B*.</u>

<u>Both</u> ideas are <u>mistaken</u>, the second more seriously misleading than the first. The first idea, on its face, is simply and wildly implausible. In general, and certainly in the case of literal statements, <u>'*A* is *B*' and '*A* is like *B*'</u> are <u>not</u> equivalent. For instance, 'Aristotle is like Plato' is true: they are both Greek, both Athenians, both philosophers, both long dead, *&c*, while 'Aristotle is Plato' is false. There is no compelling reason to think that this obvious nonequivalence disappears when '*A* is *B*' happens to be a metaphor, unless, of course, it were the case that a metaphor '*A* is *B*' is somehow, perhaps by convention, to be understood as an alternative formulation of the literal simile '*A* is like *B*', and there seems no good reason to suppose this to be the case.

<u>The second idea is that the '*A* is like *B*' associated with the metaphor '*A* is *B*' is not itself metaphorical but is literal, and as seductive as this idea has been, it is mistaken.</u> The mistake can be exposed using the useful if timeworn example 'Juliet is the

---

bibliographic guides. These are the books by Josef Stern and Roger White cited in the footnotes to this chapter's epigraphs.

sun'. If the import of Romeo's declaration were a literal comparison expressed in 'Juliet is like the sun', then the relevant comparison would be of properties literally possessed by both Juliet and the sun. There is no shortage of such properties: both Juliet and the sun occupy space, have mass, are visible, &c. But these properties are irrelevant to what Romeo hopes to communicate. What matters are these other shared properties: both Juliet and the sun are warming, they both illuminate Romeo's world, &c. And these properties—the significant ones—are indeed literal properties of the sun, but they are metaphorical properties of Juliet.]

So even if a metaphor were "reducible" to a simile or similes (already a dubious reduction), many of the most important similes themselves would also be figurative, not literal. Of course there often are literal similarities, especially in the cases I am most interested in, those in which I imagine myself to be another person. When I imagine myself to be King David, for instance, it is obviously relevant that both he and I are men, both heterosexually active, both tempted to injure others in pursuit of our own desires, and so on.

It seems obviously true that a metaphor '*A* is *B*' induces one to think of *A* as *B*, and this leads to new thoughts about *A*. How this happens is a wonderful mystery, and the ability to do it, to "see" *A* as *B*, is an indispensable human ability I am calling the talent for metaphor. This is a talent not just for making a metaphor or grasping one, not if one thinks of that only in terms of producing or understanding a single sentence. The talent is not restricted in this way: in fact it is a talent for seizing metaphors and then enlarging and altering them.

Here is a relatively elaborate metaphor from Richard Stern:[4]

> There are, I think, three very different sorts of literary experience: the writer's the reader's, and the critic's, the last two being as distinct as the first from them. . . . If we analogize the writer to an assassin, the reader is the corpse, the critic the coroner-detective.

[4] This is from his essay "Henderson's Bellow," *Kenyon Review* 21, no. 4 (1959). The essay is reprinted in a number of places, including Stern's book *One Person and Another* (Dallas: Baskerville, 1993).

This figure is a perfect illustration of two features common to metaphorical language although not always so strikingly present. First is a metaphor's capacity to suggest other, related metaphors, almost by implication. Thus if you think of a critic as someone explaining the effect of a book upon a reader, and you then think of a coroner as someone who paradigmatically explains effects, you think of the critic as a coroner, and this leads to seeing the reader as a victim and the author as his victimizer, and, although Stern does not bother to note this, it leads to thinking of the book itself as a weapon. Given this much, a competent metaphor appreciator is led to much, much more. Perhaps Tolstoy kills with large, overpowering weapons, while Proust sedates you to death. What about Hemingway? Does he use a machine gun? A sniper rifle? And then, undoubtedly, you will recall the virtually idiomatic response to a joker, "You slay me." And on and on.

But second, you may resist the metaphor or some part of it. It is extraordinary and very striking that Stern thinks of a writer as a killer.[5] If you don't see writers in that way, but are still struck by the irresistible aptness of Stern's designation of the critic as someone like a pathologist, someone seeking to understand the effect upon a reader of what he reads, then what will you do to amend Stern's figures? Perhaps you think of a novelist as a therapist, improving the muscle tone or endurance of his reader, and then the critic becomes perhaps the judge in a bodybuilding contest, or, better, a doctor who appraises your health after you submitted to the therapist he recommended, and can explain just why the therapy had this effect.

Both ways of thinking of writing metaphorically, of course, lead to the endlessly beguiling question of why the reader submits to the author's ministrations. In Stern's figure, we must ask, why does one expose oneself to an assassin? I don't know

---

[5] Stern stands by his metaphor, and has told me, "I do think of a book as a way of annihilating the reader, that is substituting the powerful structure of the book for what there before." The depth of Stern's thinking about these matters is underwritten by his being, himself, a very accomplished writer of fiction and also nonfictional essays, a critic, and a voracious reader.

Stern's answer, but I think it must be wonderful to contemplate. In the substitute figure, the question of why one goes to a therapist is less interesting, less potent, but still instructive.

Calling a writer an assassin is perhaps an uncomplimentary reference to the writer, although I doubt Stern thinks of his metaphor in this way. Many metaphors are intended, precisely, to be devices for saying negative things about their subjects.

Suppose you wish to say something uncomplimentary about Bart, and you mean to do it using a metaphor. You will say that Bart is an $X$, and the result will be an unpleasant depiction of Bart. You have to choose some noun to put in place of '$X$', and there are, surprisingly, two classes of candidates. In the more obvious choice, you will pick the name of something inherently disagreeable, say the word 'maggot'. This gives 'Bart is a maggot', a mean thing, indeed, to say when speaking of Bart. On the other hand, there is nothing intrinsically unpleasant or disagreeable about dogs, and yet if you choose 'dog' for '$X$', you will get 'Bart is a dog', which might well be an insult to Bart.

An historical example of a choice of the second kind, of something not in itself negative, is Churchill's remark about Mussolini, 'Mussolini is a utensil'.[6] There is nothing whatever negative in calling a fork or a knife or a screwdriver a utensil, but something happens when Mussolini is seen as a utensil.

There are two lessons to be learned from these examples, the first interesting but less problematic than the second. The first lesson is that whether or not metaphors have new *meanings*, and whether or not the principal use of a metaphor is to communicate the speaker's feeling about his subject, it remains true that different choices of predicates give different imports. Churchill might have called Mussolini a wolf or the devil or a parasite, but none of those has the same import as calling him a utensil.

---

[6] The remark is adapted from "Prime Minister Winston Churchill's Address to the Congress of the United States, December 26, 1941," as recorded by the British Library of Information. What Churchill said was, "The boastful Mussolini has crumpled already. He is now but a lackey and a serf, the merest utensil of his master's will."

That is, whether or not this is strictly a matter of semantics, there are relatively specific imports or depictions of ideas presented in metaphors, including those meant to insult or degrade. To think of Mussolini as a swine is to be uncomplimentary to Mussolini, no doubt, but to think of him as a utensil is, among other things, to think of him in his relation to Hitler, which is significantly more specific, and, one might say, even more accurate and informative.

The second lesson is that the mystery of metaphor—the mystery of one thing's being seen or thought of as another—is even more enigmatic than one might have expected. To see Bart as a maggot is to see Bart in a rather poor light, so to speak, but that seems to be because maggots are already in bad repute. But seeing Bart as a dog, or Mussolini as a utensil is different. Something happens when one sees Mussolini as a utensil that also puts Mussolini in a bad light, but not because of any negative association with utensils. It is Mussolini-seen-as-a-utensil that is disagreeable.

When one sees something as an $X$, one is seeing a new entity, a kind of compound. To see Bart as a maggot is to see something disagreeable, and to see anything as a maggot would be to see something disagreeable. To see Mussolini as a utensil is to see something distasteful, but not because anything seen in that way would be distasteful—for instance, one might see language as a utensil.

The overall lesson, which connects this observation to Arnold Isenberg's idea of "critical communication," is that a leading aim of many metaphor-makers is the communication of some feelings they have about the subjects of their metaphors, and the often hoped-for inducement of similar feelings in those who grasp their metaphors. Both the description, say, of Mussolini, and the attendant feeling are specific. Churchill did not want only to present Mussolini in a bad light, but to present him lit in a very specific way, and he wanted not only for us to feel negatively about *Il Duce*, but to have the feelings that go with thinking of Mussolini as a utensil. Mussolini might well also have been a swine, but that is different, a different depiction with a different attendant feeling.

Metaphorical sentences come in all forms—imperative, interrogative, and so on—but the only concern here is with those that are declarative sentences, sentences used for making statements, and among those the only interest is in those whose form is '*A* is *B*'. There are still a number of possible logical forms, for, in the first place, the 'is' may be the 'is' of predication or the 'is' of identity, and in the second place, both '*A*' and '*B*' may be either common nouns, proper nouns, or singular terms. Here are two random examples.

Yale men are poor little lambs.
Cole Porter is a poor little lamb.

The kind of metaphor I hope to exploit is the one whose subject term is a proper name or singular term, specifically either the name of a person or a singular pronoun. When the 'is' is of identity, then the form may be 'I am *N*' where '*N*' is a singular term, proper name, or definite description, something referring to a specific person. When the 'is' is of predication, the form will be 'I am a *G*', where '*G*' is a general term.

This bothersome, quasi-technical terminology can be dropped once it is clear that what I am trying to describe is what is at the center of one's thought when one imagines being someone or something other than who or what one is. It is what comes to mind when I ask,

What if I were Robert Pinsky?
What if I were a Christian?
What if I were a lover of Wagner's music?

What comes to mind, I think, are thoughts expressed in these sentences:

I am Robert Pinsky.
I am a Christian.
I am a Wagner lover.

and I construe all these sentences to be metaphors. I suppose this is a dubious construal, and many students of metaphor will find these sentences alien to their sense of metaphor. I concede that this is a novel construal, but I ask indulgence because what one must do to grasp any of these sentences is to think of one thing as something it plainly is not, and that, I think, is exactly what one must do to grasp a metaphor. Then even if it is inapt to call these sentences metaphors, the knack for grasping them is the same as the knack for grasping metaphors, and so I will call them metaphors of personal identification, and I will call the ability to grasp them the talent for metaphor.

In a metaphor of personal identification, usually, a person is said to be either another person or a person of a different kind, as in, for instance,

> Juliet is the sun.
> The Lord is my shepherd.
> The poor are the Negroes of Europe.

I will be concentrating on cases in which the person is oneself, paying most attention to the identification of oneself with another person, cases of the form 'I am $N$' where '$N$' is a singular term referring to a person. It will do to write such a case as

$$I = N, <$$

but doing so signals the need for a qualification. The '=' indicating the 'is' of identity, when used in a metaphor, is not exactly the usual relation of identity. Standard identity is a symmetric relation. Thus, $X = Y$ if and only if $Y = X$. The reason why this is not true of metaphorical identifications is this: to grasp a metaphor is to see one thing as another, and it is not, in general, the same to see $X$ as $Y$, as it is to see $Y$ as $X$.

In understanding this it may help to ponder a short story.

> A Jewish man named 'Lev', living in eastern Europe in the late nineteenth century, one day says to some friends, "If I were the Czar, I would be richer than the Czar."
>
> "How could that be?" asks his friend. "If you were the Czar, you would have all the Czar's wealth, and so you would be exactly as rich as the Czar. How could you be richer?"
>
> "Well," says Lev, "if I were the Czar, on the side I would give Hebrew lessons."

What's wrong with this? Is anything wrong with it?

Well, for a start, the Czar wouldn't give Hebrew lessons because, in the first place, it's just not something the Czar would do, and, secondly, it's not something the Czar could do, because, of course, the Czar doesn't know the language. But of course Lev knows Hebrew, and in fact right now he does make a little money giving Hebrew lessons.

So, would you say that if the Czar were Lev, he would be even richer? Does that seem different from asking, what if Lev were the Czar?

Do you feel like saying either of these?

> If Lev were the Czar, he wouldn't know Hebrew.
> If the Czar were Lev, he would know Hebrew.

My topic is the phenomenon of understanding one another, and, as noted earlier, it may seem dubious to connect this topic with the topic of metaphor. I do not know to what length the comparison can be kept salient, but I make the comparison, provisionally but also polemically, for this reason: the creation, expression, and comprehension of metaphors must involve speaking and thinking of one thing as another. I am persuaded that understanding one another involves thinking of oneself as another, and thus the talent for doing this must be related to the talent for thinking of one thing as another; and it may be the same talent, differently deployed. Thus I have tried taking sentences like 'Lev is the Czar', 'The Czar is Lev', and 'I am Lev' as metaphors. I will continue to do that.

Treating these "personal identifications" as metaphors may well seem unusual, and even suspect, and so, perhaps, will my very broad conception of metaphor. I am using the term to cover an array of forms, in all of which one thing is regarded as something that it is not. This sense comprehends metaphors in the usual, narrow sense, as well as figurative similes, analogies, allegories, and possibly even what might more commonly be regarded as parables.[7]

---

[7] As extravagant as this idea may seem, I am not alone in entertaining it. In his essay "Midrash and Allegory," Gerald L. Bruns notes that "the logic of allegory is the same as in metaphor as regards the truth of statements or propo-

In a metaphor *A* is said to be *B*, in a simile *A* is said to be like *B*, in an analogy *A* is said to stand to *C* as *B* stands to *D* (and in some cases *C* and *D* are the same, as in "God is to me as my father is to me," and there may be cases in which *A* and *B* are the same), while in allegory, typically, only *B* is mentioned and it is left to the reader to understand that *B* stands for, or represents, or "allegorizes" *A.* For examples we can consider, respectively, "Juliet is the sun," "My love is like a red, red rose," "Juliet stands to other women as the sun to the moon," and, for an allegory of sorts, those lines in the *Song of Songs* in which a man and a woman make physical love when those lines are reunderstood either, as with Christians, to stand for the relation of Jesus to the Church, or, as with Jews, to stand for the relation of God to the people of Israel.

In every case, so I think, the figure is grounded in the idea that *A* can be understood (or "seen") as *B*, and in virtually every interesting case this will be not because *A* and *B* share some property but because *B* has some property that *A* can be thought of as having, or imagined to have, when in fact the property is not literally a property of *A*.

During a reading he gave in Chicago when he was the honoree at Poetry Day 2006, Robert Hass said, "Someone had proposed to me that I should write a sequence of poems that were in succession simile, metaphor, and allegory." He then read this:

THREE DAWN SONGS IN SUMMER[8]

*1.*

The first long shadows in the fields
Are like mortal difficulty.
The first birdsong is not like that at all.

---

sitions" (Robert Alter and Frank Kermode, editors, *The Literary Guide to the Bible* [Cambridge, MA: Harvard University Press, 1987]).

[8] The poem is printed in Hass's collection *Time and Materials* (New York: Harper-Collins, 2007).

### 2.

The light in summer is very young and wholly
  unsupervised.
No one has made it sit down to breakfast.
It's the first one up, the first one out.

### 3.

Because he has opened his eyes, he must be light
And she, sleeping beside him, must be the visible,
One ringlet of hair curled about her ear.
Into which he whispers, "Wake up!"
"Wake up!" he whispers.

What happens when one person is (metaphorically) identified with another is especially well illustrated when the biblical
David is entangled in such an identification, but before turning
to that story I will take up a more mundane example in order
to make clear why metaphorical identity is not symmetrical,
and is therefore not literal identity, and also to illustrate the
ubiquity of metaphors of human understanding in even the
most pedestrian exchanges.

# CHAPTER TWO

## *Being a Good Sport*

Definition of *fair play*: upright conduct in a game; equity
in the conditions or opportunities afforded to a player.
—*Oxford English Dictionary*

THINKING of one person as another is a bemusing and mysterious enterprise, but if I am right, the ability to do this is a
fundamental human capacity without which our moral and aes-
thetic lives would scarcely be possible. This book is an attempt
to gain some preliminary understanding of the dimensions of
this topic.

To see the asymmetry of such identification, and this time
with a faint moral overtone not present in the story of Lev and
the Czar, consider the kind of admonition frequently addressed
to children.

The question arises what Abner would do (or how Abner
would feel) in some situation. I might approach this question
by asking any of these:

1. What would Abner do? (How would Abner feel?)
2. What would I do?
3. What would I do if I were Abner?
4. What would Abner do if he were me?

The answers to all these questions might be the same, but
they might all be different from one another, or at least so I
think. It may be that Abner is some other man, but it may be
that Abner is a fictional character, an author (or other artist),

or, perhaps, in a case that arises out of consideration of #3 and #4, it may be that Abner is me considered in circumstances other than my own.

The first two questions, 'What would Abner do?' and 'What would I do?', seem straightforward and unproblematic, requiring no particular feat of imagination to answer, and so they may be, but I will note that one might be able to give a better answer to one of the questions than to the other. That is, I may be better able to say what Abner would do than to say what I would do. There are cases, familiar if uncommon, in which I know relevantly more about Abner than about myself. For instance, if Abner is a battle-tried and -hardened soldier who has exhibited exemplary bravery and calm when under fire, and I am someone who has lived his entire life out of harm's way, then if it is asked how either of us will behave when we are in combat being shot at, I am likely to be more confident in predicting how Abner will react than in saying what I will do. I may be brave, I may be terrified and unable to stand my ground. I just don't know, while I have good reasons for predicting Abner's reaction. In general, however, obviously, I am likelier to know myself than I am to know Abner, and so I expect to do better answering how I would act.

With these questions, what seems to be required is a prediction, and even if I can predict Abner's actions and feelings better than I can predict my own, and even if prediction can be a difficult undertaking, predicting seems to be all that is involved. With the other two questions, however, 'What would I do if I were Abner?' and 'What would Abner do if he were me?', even if answering is ultimately a matter of predicting, there is a prior requirement, namely that one do something like imagine the person about whom the prediction is to be made. The person whose actions or feelings are to be predicted is either *Abner-if-he-were-me* or *me-if-I-were-Abner*, and I will have to gain a sense of this person if I am to make guesses about what he would do. I would like to say something about how this sense is gained.

The first thing to note is that even if something like an identity statement is involved, it is not simply that. It is not just

'Abner = me'. To see this, it will do, I think, to consider a case in which I am not involved but which we might address, so to speak, from outside.

Bart has done something to Abner you think he shouldn't have done. You remonstrate, but which of these do you say?

5. "How would you like it if the person that were done to were you?" [*A* = *B*.]

or

6. "How would you like that if you were Abner?" [*B* = *A*.]

Either way, you are asking Bart to imagine something, but I think that #5 and #6 are different imaginings. It may not be as easy as one thinks to imagine how one would feel or act under certain conditions, and so it may not be so easy for Bart to answer honestly the question of how he would like it if this thing happened to him; but it is different—and probably yet harder—for him to answer the question of how he would like it if he were Abner and it happened to him.

You may think that answering #5 and #6 are not so different, but you must admit that they are not the same, for the simple reason that the answers given could easily be different. Suppose Bart is the kind of game-player who enjoys taunting and being taunted by his opponent. So he talks trash to his opponent, the gentle, well-mannered, good sport Abner. You are upset by Bart's conduct and you ask a version of questions #5 and #6. Well, Bart might well reply to the #5 version, "As a matter of fact, I would like it very much if Abner taunted me; in fact I thrive on such talk." But to the #6 version Bart must reply differently, I think, because he knows Abner does not at all like being taunted. It adversely affects his play of the game, and reduces him to tears. Please do not think I believe it is easy to answer the question "How would you feel if you were Abner?" despite the example I have just given. It is the main burden of this essay to find some entrée into the sense of the idea that I am Abner, or whatever idea I must entertain if I am to answer questions of the kind that begin 'If you were Abner . . .'.

Here I am noting only that answering this question is different from answering the question of how I would feel if it were done to me.

What happens when I ask what if I were Abner, or what if Abner were me? I have been trying to get a grip on this question by supposing, at least tentatively, that what is involved is a metaphor, a metaphorical proposition that is a kind of identity statement. [1] I did this because it seemed—and seems—to me that thinking of myself as Abner, or of Abner as me, is an achievement very much like that which goes with grasping a metaphor.

Not every response to another requires imagining oneself to be that other. This seems obvious. I might very well be moved to do something to alleviate your pain or augment your pleasure, or do any number of other things, without having first to imagine being the recipient of such an effort. For instance, you tell me that it pains you to hear certain sounds, and I then turn off those sounds without ever trying or having to try to imagine having such an affliction. It is perhaps interesting that just this kind of interaction often occurs when one of the participants is not human. I recall my dog, the late and much lamented Dr. Smith, being greatly annoyed and seemingly even in pain, when I did certain things while trimming his nails. I had no clear idea, either in reality or imagination, just what he was feeling, but I was moved to stop what I was doing.

The kind of interpersonal imagining this book is concerned with is called into play only on some occasions, and with certain special urgencies at hand, and I have absolutely no wish to claim that such efforts of empathy are always involved. If this book goes wrong, it will not be because I claim that such interpersonal connection is always required, but because I am wrong to claim that it is sometimes required. Furthermore, it may well be that a decent human response, say to someone's pain, might be moved in one person by his felt connection with the sufferer,

---

[1] I introduced this idea briefly in "Metaphor, Feeling, and Narrative," *Philosophy and Literature* 21, no. 2 (October, 1997), pp. 223–44, and began to develop it in "Identifying with Metaphor: Metaphors of Personal Identification," *The Journal of Aesthetics and Art Criticism* 57, no. 4 (Fall, 1999), pp. 399–409.

while another Samaritan responds simply because he believes someone is in pain while having no imaginative sense whatever of just what that pain is.

So I am claiming only that some times, for some people, in some circumstances, it is incumbent upon one to attempt metaphorical identification. Which are those times, those people, those circumstances? I do not think any rule can be given for this.

# CHAPTER THREE

## *From the Bible: Nathan and David*

> [David] masters the harp as well as the sword: a poet
> as well as a warrior-killer, but as a poet he is far above
> any other hero, and as a killer no one among the
> poets can even approach him.
> —ROBERT PINSKY [1]

> Nathan's rhetorical trap has now snapped shut.
> David, by his access of anger, condemns himself,
> and he is now the helpless target of the denunciation
> that Nathan will unleash.
> —ROBERT ALTER[2]

HERE is a story that concludes with an explicit metaphor of personal identification.

With his army away besieging the Ammonite city of Rabbah, King David has remained at home, in his palace. One morning as he is walking on the roof of the palace, David sees a young woman in her bath in a courtyard next door. David learns that she is Bathsheba, wife of Uriah, who is one of his soldiers. Struck by her beauty, David summons Bathsheba to him at the palace and sleeps with her. When she becomes pregnant, David sends a message to his military commander Joab, telling him to send Uriah to David. When Uriah returns from the war and makes a report to David, David urges him to spend the night

---

[1] *The Life of David* (New York: Schocken, 2005).
[2] *The David Story* (New York: W. W. Norton, 1999).

with his wife Bathsheba. David's hope, of course, is that Bathsheba's pregnancy will be credited to her husband Uriah. But
Uriah spends the night alone, sleeping outdoors, and when
David asks why, Uriah says he should not go home and be with
his wife when Joab and the armies of Judah and Israel, accompa-
nied by the ark, are all campaigning in the field. David keeps
Uriah in Jerusalem one more night, wining and dining him,
and indeed getting him drunk, but Uriah again abstains from
going home. Then David sends an instruction to Joab: Joab is
to set Uriah among a group of soldiers engaged in fierce fighting near the wall of Rabbah. When the fighting becomes especially dangerous, Joab is to withdraw from behind Uriah. Joab
follows these instructions, Uriah is left unsupported and is
killed, and Joab reports the events to David. David then summons the widowed Bathsheba to live in the palace. The Lord
is displeased with what David has done, says the author of the
book, and the author goes on:

> And the Lord sent Nathan unto David. And he came unto him,
> and said unto him, There were two men in one city, the one rich,
> and the other poor.
>
> The rich man had exceeding many flocks and herds:
>
> But the poor man had nothing, save one little ewe lamb, which
> he had bought and nourished up: and it grew up together with
> him, and with his children; it did eat of his own meat, and drank of
> his own cup, and lay in his bosom, and was unto him as a daughter.
>
> And there came a traveler unto the rich man, and he spared to
> take of his own flock and of his own herd, to dress for the wayfar-
> ing man that was come unto him; but took the poor man's lamb,
> and dressed it for the man that was come to him.
>
> And David's anger was greatly kindled against the man; and he
> said to Nathan, As the Lord liveth, the man that hath done this
> thing shall surely die:
>
> And he shall restore the lamb fourfold, because he did this
> thing, and because he had no pity.
>
> And Nathan said to David, Thou art the man.[3]

[3] Quoted from 2 Samuel, chapter 12 in the King James translation. The
precedent events are recounted in chapter 11.

What has happened here, between Nathan the prophet and David the king? Two fundamental controlling points seem clear: (1) Nathan has not told David anything David did not already know; (2) when Nathan has finished speaking, David has new feelings and thoughts about something he has already known. How does Nathan bring this about?

How can David not have known that he was rich in wives while Uriah had only Bathsheba? But David took Bathsheba anyway, and he has shown no contrition. What has Nathan done about this?

Of course Nathan has told David about the rich man and the poor man's ewe lamb, but that is not something known to Nathan or David, because that story is not true. Even if it were true, it would make no difference, because the efficacy of the story does not depend upon the story's being true. It depends only upon David's entertaining the story sufficiently to begin to have feelings about the poor man and the rich man.

What has happened is something like this. David's anger and moral outrage at the rich man have been transferred to himself. Nathan says "You are the man," which is essentially "You, David, are the rich man who has taken a poor man's only ewe lamb," and David connects.

If Nathan's story tells David nothing new, then how does it work its effect? Perhaps we should say that Nathan does tell something new to David. He tells David that it is possible to see—that indeed Nathan does see—David in his treatment of Uriah and Bathsheba as a rich man taking a poor man's only ewe lamb; and when the story has been told, David himself sees David in that way. When David sees himself in that way, his sense of himself is changed. Feelings about himself arise that had not arisen before. How does this happen? We should not settle for an easy answer. It is not a simple matter of similarity. No doubt David "is like" the rich man in the story. But that itself leads to nothing. What matters is that some specific feeling attached to David's sense of the rich man is provoked in David's sense of himself, to whom it had not previously been attached. This is not achieved simply by drawing David's attention to the fact that he and the rich man share membership in some similarity class. Nathan needs the absolute particularity of the rich man. That is what arouses David's feelings. Nathan does not effect the transfer of feeling by saying "You resemble people whom you dislike." David might accept the proposition that he is like these disagreeable people and yet not be moved to anger at himself. After all, any group can be judged similar in some respect or other, and the question will remain, why should David identify himself as such a person with respect to his feelings? Nathan does not permit this way out. Instead of telling David that he resembles people who make him angry, Nathan says, with absolute specificity and particularity, that David is the rich man, exactly the man at whom he is angry. And David responds at once.

To understand Nathan's achievement, his effect upon David, one can do no better than invoke an idea of Arnold Isenberg's. [4] He wished to understand just what could be happening, and what in fact does happen, when the critic of some piece of art, having offered a judgment of the work's value, then points to some property of the work. In an astonishingly brief and effective argument, Isenberg undermined the common idea that the citation of the work's property could function as a *reason* in support of the value judgment. He then went on to offer a deep and beautiful conception of what, in fact, such a critic might accomplish, given that the critic could not be presenting a logically sound argument in favor of his judgment.

What the critic must hope, Isenberg thought, is that by drawing attention to properties of the work, he might induce in his audience a similar view of the work; that is, in Isenberg's felicitous phrase, that he might achieve a "sameness of vision" in his audience. This sameness of vision might or might not be followed by a "community of feeling." What he meant by this is that when you, the critic, have made your best attempt to get me to see in the work what you do, if your attempt has suc-

---

[4] Isenberg's essay "Critical Communication" was published in *Philosophical Review* 58, no. 4 (July, 1949). It has been reprinted in a number of places, including *Aesthetics and the Theory of Criticism: Selected Essays of Arnold Isenberg* (Chicago: University of Chicago Press, 1973).

ceeded, then I, now seeing the work as you do, might or might not feel about it as you do.

If there has been a better description—especially a better brief description—of the ambition and sometime achievement of art criticism than this one of Isenberg's, I do not know it. There are two implications, or amplifications, of Isenberg's description that he did not note, to which I draw your attention.

First, and only in passing, is the obvious fact that this dynamic of attempted community of feeling applies just as well in cases that have nothing to do with art. It applies when you attempt to get me to join you in delight at the colors of the setting sun, or in disgust at someone's overly scanty clothing. It may also apply when you are enlisting my joy, delight, disgust, or nausea in the contemplation of a person or a person's behavior.

Second, and critically for the thesis that underlies much of this book, is the fact that this description of Isenberg's of the search for sameness and community is a brilliant description of the use of metaphor. When your metaphor is '$X$ is $Y$', you are hoping that I will see $X$ as you do, namely as $Y$, and, most likely, although your proximate aim is to get me to see $X$ is this way, your ultimate wish is that I will feel about $X$ as you do.

Nathan has presented David with the metaphor 'David is the rich man', and Nathan's success is an Isenbergian achievement. Nathan achieves a community of feeling (between himself and David) by inducing in David a sameness of vision (with Nathan himself, a sameness in the way they now see David's treatment of Uriah). Indeed there is a kind of double community created. First, David and Nathan now both feel the same about David's treatment of Uriah, and, second, David now feels about himself as he feels about the rich man. I do not know how to analyze the proposition that, after the story, David sees himself as the rich man of the story, and I am not sure that any analysis is to be given. That David does now see in this way is proved, in the only way these things can be proved, by the fact that he now feels about himself as he already felt about the rich man. It is the feeling that anchors the metaphor and signals its success. And this similarity of feeling (the similarity between David's feeling about the rich man, and his newly arisen feeling about himself) is the only similarity that matters, and it might be as well to say that this is not a similarity of feeling, but an identity. Nathan says "You are the rich man," and David's implicit response is "Yes, and I loathe myself as I loathe the rich man."

In this similarity, a similarity in feeling, there may be an opportunity to credit a well-known remark of Max Black's:

> It would be more illuminating in some of these cases to say that the metaphor creates the similarity than to say that it formulates some similarity antecedently existing.[5]

This remark has appealed to many authors, including Nelson Goodman, and many have endorsed it; but it is difficult to make it plausible if the similarity in question is one between properties of two objects (as Black intended it). If we are concerned with feelings, however, then the remark is entirely sensible, because the second feeling (in this case, David's feeling about his own actions) is called into existence by the metaphor, and therewith its similarity to the original feeling (in this case, David's feeling about the actions of the rich man).

As long as I am engaged in what may well seem to you flights of figure and fancy, I will stray from my official topic to draw your attention to another feature of Nathan's story. Nathan's story itself occurs within a story, a story known to us as 'The Second Book of Samuel'. We may suppose that story, too, has its author, and that author stands to someone—say us—as Nathan stands to David. Given how we understand Nathan's story to David, how are we to understand this author's story to us? What does Nathan want of David? What does the author want of us? This is a delightful exercise, which you will be happy I am leaving for you, save for two points I urge attention to. The first is the deep, striking peculiarity in the direction of David's connection. I am more horrified by David's theft of Bathsheba and murder of Uriah than I am by the rich man's conscription of the ewe lamb and treatment of the poor man. To arouse my ire at the rich man you might tell me that he is David taking

[5] Max Black, "Metaphor," *Proceedings of the Aristotelian Society*, N. S. 55 (1954–55), pp. 284–85.

Uriah's only wife. But with David the feeling flows the other way. This is a salient difference between me and David, king of Israel; and it is a vital fact about David that he has deep, direct, immediate feelings about simple human matters, and these feelings must be infused into his thoughts about his imperial self.[6] Perhaps we should not be surprised by this peculiarity in David's sensibility, given what we know of David. Although David is a warrior and man of action, like his predecessor Saul, and unlike his own son Solomon, and he is politically astute, like Solomon but unlike Saul, he is also something else: he has the soul and imagination of an artist. Remember that David is a dancer, a singer, and a poet, and this may be why, in more than one instance, he is reached by the art of literary invention.

In telling the story of a story, the author of the books of Samuel leaves me to observe a difference between David and me, and thus a striking fact about David. I have no wish here to open questions concerning readers' "identification" with characters in stories they read, but I will—innocuously, I hope—raise the question of which of a story's characters the reader feels himself most like. When you read the book of Jeremiah, for instance, and you read of Jeremiah's complaints about his fellow citizens, do you feel more like Jeremiah or more like one of the recipients of his incessant harangues? When you read the book of Exodus, do you feel like Moses or like Aaron or like one of the backsliding emigrants pining for the comforts of Egypt? Whose side would you have been on, had you been in one of those stories? It is not obvious, at least not for me. But here, in the case of Nathan's address to David, I am clear. I find David's actions appalling, much worse than the miserly action of the rich man, and I can imagine trying to persuade the rich man of his shame by telling him the story of David and

---

[6] Another striking example is to be found two chapters later, when Joab seeks to reconcile David with his son Absalom, after Absalom has killed his half-brother Amnon and then run away from David's expected wrath. Joab sends a woman of Tekoa to tell David a story. David reacts strongly to the story, and then is told that the story that seemed to be about the woman and her sons is in fact about David and his sons.

Uriah, and expecting him to see himself as David. But David is not like that. For him, the selfishness of the rich man excites his feeling, and he must connect himself to that. Thus the author of the book of Samuel, along with everything else done in that magnificent text, shows something profoundly important about David, as the author shows that I cannot easily identify myself with David.

The second point sounds heretical, I suppose, but I do not mean it as such: I mean it as a practical point about the power of the Second Book of Samuel. A salient question about any story is, is it true? Earlier I said that Nathan's story about the rich man and the poor man is not true, but I am not sure of that. The surrounding text does not settle the question, nor even address it. Does Nathan know of such a pair, one rich and one poor, who carried on in that way? It is possible that he does, although my sense of Nathan's story is that he is making it up. The critical point is that it does not matter, at least with regard to the story's capacity to move David and to instruct him, the person to whom the story is told. When he hears it, no doubt, David takes the story to be true; but when he realizes the story has been told in order to say something about David, then what? We are not told whether David continues to believe in the existence of the rich and poor men of the story, and we need not be told, because with regard to David's new sense of himself, it does not matter.

Before I leave this topic, the instruction of David by Nathan, I will mention one more layer in its story of interpersonal identification. At the very start, when Nathan tells David of the rich man and the poor man, how is it that David's initial anger is kindled? When he hears what the rich man has done, is it because David thinks of himself as the poor man that he feels anger at the rich man? If so, then the entire transaction is an amazing movement, with David first thinking of himself as the poor man, angry at the rich man, and then of himself as the rich man, the fit object of that anger. But I will go no further, and I leave it for you to follow the path of David's route to self-understanding.

What shall we think of the containing story, the story called 'The Second Book of Samuel'? That story is read as true by many readers of the Bible, it is read as fictional literature by many others, and by some it is read agnostically. I think the story is meant to instruct. Its author aims to inspire feelings and actions in her readers, and—at least in this respect—her success does not seem to depend upon whether the story is true, or even whether it is regarded as true by its readers.[7]

The story has the capacity to excite feelings about its characters, and when the reader accepts a (metaphorical) assertion that he or someone else is one of those characters, he may find himself with a new feeling about people—perhaps himself— who are real people outside the story, whether or not the people in the story are real. Stories move us, excite us, instruct us, and, in the first instance, in the dynamics of this effect, it does not seem to matter whether the story is thought to be true.

[7] In referring to the author of the books of Samuel I use the feminine pronoun 'she'. I do this because of Ms. Adrien J. Bledstein, my first and best Bible teacher. When teaching these books Ms. Bledstein ventured the hypothesis that they were written by a woman living in the house of David; in fact that they were written by Tamar. I am incompetent to have an opinion in this matter of authorship, but my respect and affection for Ms. Bledstein lead me to offer her this token.

# CHAPTER FOUR

## *Real Feelings, Unreal People*

Imaginary gardens with real toads in them . . .
—MARIANNE MOORE[1]

You may not believe me, but I've always liked you,
Hank. You're like a character in a good book.
Almost real, you know?
—A character in RICHARD RUSSO's novel, *Straight Man*[2]

After the last sentence is read, the reader continues to
see Russo's tender, messed-up people coming out of
doorways, lurching through life. And keeps on seeing
them because they are as real as we are.
—E. ANNIE PROULX[3]

SURELY it makes a difference whether the character for whom
one has feelings is thought to be real, and yet it is not so clear
just what difference it makes. It is tempting to suppose that
when a thing is fictional, either we can have no feelings about
it, or our feelings are peculiar and are not the feelings we would
have if the thing were real. There is some truth in this supposition, but in the main it is misleading.

In the first place, the mere thought of something is the same
whether the thing is real or not, and this fact has been clear at

[1] From the poem "Poetry."
[2] (New York: Random House, 1997), p. 106.
[3] Jacket blurb for *Straight Man*.

least since Kant's analysis of the "ontological" argument for the existence of God.

But then what of the feelings attached to the thought of something, and what happens to those feelings when the thinker believes the thing is not real? It might be argued that my feelings about a fiction cannot be the same as my feelings about something real because my feelings do not lead me to the same actions in both cases, but this would be too hasty a conclusion. Consider the feeling of fear, for instance, an example discussed in recent philosophy of art. Suppose I experience fear when watching Roman Polanski's *Chinatown*: I am afraid that the character Mrs. Mulwray (Faye Dunaway) will be hurt.

Why deny that this is real, genuine fear on my part? There seem to be two reasons: first, if I truly feared for the lady, I would at least try to do something to save her; and second, since fear is an unpleasant experience, I would avoid seeing *Chinatown* and thereby avoid the unpleasantness.

These seem to be what you would expect of someone in a situation in which he experienced fear, that he would try to change things, or withdraw from the situation, or, in a phrase, that he would try to stop being afraid. That seems right, but in fact it is wrong as a general point, as can be seen as soon as we consider activities like bullfighting, automobile racing, mountain climbing, and boxing, for instance. In all these enterprises there is significant danger, and that fearsome danger is integral to the experience. Remove the danger—say, with a mechanical bull—and the experience will be severely altered for both participants and spectators, altered to a point at which almost all interest will be lost. The danger is there, and so is the fear it inspires. Of course the bullfighter is afraid of being gored, perhaps to death, and the race driver is afraid of crashing, perhaps fatally, and the mountaineer is afraid of falling, freezing, and suffocating. Call these adventurers *fearless* if you like, but not if that means without fear. They are brave people, and as Aristotle put it, a brave person is not someone without fear, but is someone who can go on despite his fear.

What of the spectator at such an event? Surely there is no difficulty in crediting him too with fear, fear that the participant will fall victim to exactly what the participant himself is afraid of. But what if the participant and his danger are fictional: then what does the spectator feel? I may fear for a bullfighter in a bullring in Madrid, but how can I fear for Mrs. Mulwray in *Chinatown*? I do not know *how* I can do that, nor do I know that there should be a question, but I am sure that I do.

An instructive example is that of the sports fan, the follower, say, of a baseball team. A fan takes on a range of pleasures and pains otherwise unavailable. Anyone would fear for the crash of an automobile racer or the goring of a matador, but there is nothing intrinsically frightening in the loss of a game by the Chicago White Sox. But I do fear such a loss. That fear—the fear of a loss to the Cubs during interleague play—is predicated upon one's being a fan of the White Sox, caring how they fare. As it happens, I satisfy that precondition, but there is nothing in the nature of my bare humanity that makes it so. Besides being a human being capable of sympathy and empathy, I had also to come to *care* for the White Sox. How one becomes a fan is not easy to say. Sometimes it is a complex development, and frequently it is not a matter of choice, but however it has come about, once one is fan, one is *engaged*. It is possible to watch and enjoy a baseball game or any contest, sporting or otherwise, without being engaged, without caring about the outcome. Such a spectator can enjoy the play, admire the virtuosity, and generally take pleasure in the event, and such a spectator will not fear a loss by either contestant. The fan, however, is exactly an engaged spectator, and the measure of his engagement is precisely the strength of his fear of a loss. This is such an important part of spectatorship that some of us, when witnessing a contest, inevitably "take sides." I watch a tennis match between players I know nothing of, or I watch a soccer match despite my having virtually no interest in soccer, or I watch an installment of the television quiz contest *Jeopardy*, and I find myself coming to hope for the success of one of the contestants and thus to fear that contestant's failure.

A sports match is a real thing, of course, even if one's engagement in its outcome has to be willed, and the events of a fiction, by definition, are not real; and yet the phenomenon of being a fan is instructive, for it shows the human capacity to come to *care* about things that are not in and of themselves matters of concern.

Let us turn back to fiction, to two examples, each of which comes with descriptions of the feelings it arouses.

During the 1940's, Thomas Mann, in exile from Germany, was living in southern California. Among his companions were a number of other émigré Germans, and they, together with a number of Americans, spent many evenings together, during which the writers often read to one another from the books they were working on. After 1945 Mann was occupied writing *Doctor Faustus*, and in his diary notes from that period, he records two occasions upon which people read or heard the chapter from that book in which a child dies. Here is what he says (the child's name is 'Nepomuk'; his nickname is 'Echo'):

New Year's Day 1947 brought me a true joy. In the morning I had finished the cantata chapter, though this ending was to be revised. A few days before, I had sent Erika in New York the parts of the manuscript she had not yet seen, about ten chapters for her to check. Now, upon my return from a walk, I found to my mild alarm an announcement of a telegram "not to be telephoned." It was fetched, and read in English: "Read all night. Shall go into new year reddened eyes but happy heart. Wondering only how on earth you do it. Thanks, congratulations, etc." What a joy to my heart this characteristic utterance of the dear child! I had known, I suppose, that she would weep over Echo. What had happened, as she told me soon afterwards, contained far more of life's comedy that I had imagined. It seemed that after reading all night she had, in honor of the new year, submitted herself to the care of a beauty shop. In the afternoon, while reading the Echo chapter, the whole of her artful make-up, mascara and all, had been washed away by tears and flowed in black streaks over her face. [p. 226]

We spent the evening with the Alfred Neumanns and drank champagne to toast the completion of a work to which this good friend had contributed so much. After the coffee I read the Echo chapter. Everyone was much moved. Kitty, so we heard next day, was unable to sleep that night, so strongly was she affected by the death of the child. [p. 232][4]

In these remarks Mann is no doubt testifying to the strength and effectiveness of his own writing, but he is also ingenuously recording two events, both told to him, one by someone who has read the Echo chapter herself, and one who has heard it read, and he is telling us that both women, Mann's daughter and Neumann's wife, were greatly upset by the death of the child. There is no suggestion that their sorrow and grief were not *real* sorrow and grief. Is that because Mann is not attending to an important "philosophical" distinction to be made between real-life, real-world feelings and those feelings inspired by fiction? I do not think so, because I have no commitment to the distinction.

I do not remember just how I felt when reading of Echo's death in *Doctor Faustus*, and so I offer another example, one for which I can attest to my own feelings, past and present.

Here is a passage from Sholokhov's *And Quiet Flows the Don*. This is a multi-character novel, beginning around the time of World War I and continuing through Russia's civil war, when the Don Cossacks found themselves divided between the Reds and the Whites, thus often fighting against one another, including people they knew personally. The main character is Grigory Panteleyevich Melekhov, and it is with him that the story begins and ends. His older brother is Pyotr Panteleyevich Melekhov. In this passage Pyotr's group of Cossacks has been cornered by an enemy group, some of them known to Pyotr, and the enemy have called on those they've trapped to come out and surrender.

> With a terrible effort Pyotr shook off his lethargy. He thought he had detected a sneer in the words "let you go." He shouted hoarsely: "Back!" But no one listened to him. All the Cossacks except Antip crawled out of the gully.

[4] Thomas Mann, *The Story of a Novel: The Genesis of Doctor Faustus*, translated from the German by Richard and Clara Winston (New York, Alfred A. Knopf, 1961).

He was the last to emerge. Within him, like a babe below a
woman's heart, life was stirring powerfully. The instinct for self-
preservation had prompted him to remove the bullets from his rifle
magazine before he climbed up the steep slope. His eyes were
muddy, his heart filled his chest. He was choking like a child in
heavy sleep. He tore his collar open. His eyes were filled with sweat,
his hands slipped over the cold slope of the cliff. Panting, he clam-
bered to the spot where they were standing, threw his rifle down
at his feet, and raised his hands above his head. The Cossacks who
had come out before him were huddled close together. Mikhail
Koshevoi stepped out of the group of Red foot and horse soldiers
and strode towards them. He went up to Pyotr and, standing right
in front of him, his eyes fixed on the ground, asked quietly:

"Had enough of fighting?" He waited a moment for an answer,
then, still staring at Pyotr's feet, asked in the same tone: "You
were in command of them, weren't you?"

Pyotr's lips quivered. With a gesture of terrible weariness, with
great difficulty he raised his hand to his wet brow. Mikhail's long
eyelashes flickered, his swollen upper lip curled. His body was
shaken with such a violent shudder that it seemed he would not
be able to keep his feet. But he at once raised his eyes to Pyotr's,
gazed straight into his pupils, piercing them with a strangely alien
gaze, and muttered hurriedly:

"Undress!"

Pyotr quickly threw off his sheepskin jacket, carefully rolled it
up, and laid it on the snow. He removed his cap, his belt, his khaki
shirt, and, sitting on the end of his jacket, began to pull off his
boots, turning paler every moment.

Ivan Alexeyevich dismounted and came across to them, gritting
his teeth in fear of bursting into tears.

"Don't take off your shirt," Mikhail whispered, and, shud-
dering, shouted abruptly:

"Quicker, you . . ."

Pyotr hastily thrust his woolen stockings into the tops of his
boots and, straightening up, stepped off his coat with his bare feet,
a saffron yellow against the snow.

Hardly moving his lips, Pyotr called to Ivan Alexeyevich:
"Cousin!" Ivan stood watching silently as the snow melted under

Pyotr's bare feet. "Cousin Ivan, you were the godfather of my child. . . . Cousin, don't shoot me," Pyotr pleaded. Seeing Mikhail had already raised his revolver to the level of his chest, he dilated his eyes as though expecting a dazzling flash, and drew his head down into his shoulders.

He did not hear the shot; he fell headlong, as though someone had struck him a violent blow.

It seemed to him that Koshevoi's outstretched hand seized his heart and squeezed the blood from him. With a last effort Pyotr threw open the collar of his shirt and lay bare the bullet hole under his left nipple. At first the blood oozed slowly from the wound; then, finding vent, it spurted up in a thick dark stream.[5]

I first read the book many years ago; this was my experience, more or less, when I read the passage just quoted: When Pyotr and his troops were cornered, I was not especially concerned, probably because I had no particular allegiance to the Whites or the Reds; but I began to be frightened as I realized, from what had happened earlier, that the Cossacks who'd been captured might be executed. This bothered me because I had developed a liking for Pyotr, and I had hoped that both he and his brother Grigory would survive the war. I became progressively more worried as I read on, and I was extremely upset when Pyotr was ordered to remove his clothing. I held out some hope that the clothing was simply being stolen, for use by his enemies, but I knew that he was perhaps being told to take off his coat so that it would not be damaged by a bullet. This, of course, proved true, and I then felt distress and sadness when I read the beautiful, devastating description of his execution. I still wish it hadn't happened.

It seems to me now, as it seemed to me when I first read Sholokhov, that I feel genuine fear, apprehension, sadness, and grief, and I am unconvinced that there is any compelling reason to deny that I did, and do. Here are some of the (less than compelling) reasons, and my reasons for rejecting them.

[5] Mikhail Sholokhov, *And Quiet Flows the Don*, translated by Stephen Garry, revised and completed by Robert Daglish (Moscow: Foreign Languages Publishing House, no date given), book 3, chapter 33.

Perhaps one thinks that if I were genuinely afraid on behalf of a real Pyotr in the real world, I would have done something or at least tried to do something to save him. But this needn't be true. Suppose that the passage from Sholokhov were a description of a real-world event, and I were there to witness it. Suppose I were watching things unfold from a hiding place, unseen myself but able to see everything happening, and aware that there was absolutely nothing I could do to save Pyotr. Or suppose I were watching from a quarter mile away, looking through powerful binoculars. In either case I would do nothing *because there would be nothing I could do.* And now let us acknowledge that something's being fictional is itself simply one reason why I can do nothing, if a rather special and unusual reason.

Still, one says, in the real world, if it were possible for me to intervene, I would. Fine, because I think that if I could affect what happens in the passage narrating Pyotr's death, I would.

It may seem that I have gone over this too briskly, and although I think there is little more to be said, it may be good to go over it once more, this time a little more systematically.

With regard to our feelings about fictions there are two opposed assumptions, or intuitions.

1. One cannot have real feelings about things known not to exist, or at least the feelings one does have are not the same as the feelings one has about real, existent things.
2. Ordinary readers, and extraordinary ones as well, do commonly say they are having real feelings about fictions, and they name these feelings with the same words they use when naming feelings they have about real, existent things.

It is not clear how to adjudicate between these two basic intuitions, but it is clear to me that (2) has a certain priority, and that it is up to a proponent of (1) to show that (2) is not decisive. I think this in part because I am a largely unreconstructed advocate of what was once called "ordinary language philosophy," but also because of this: people who speak without qualification of their real feelings for fictions, and do so in words also used for feelings about real things, perfectly well understand one another when they speak in this way, and they do not mislead either one another or anyone else. Thus it seems to me that if they are in error, or are speaking mistakenly either through carelessness or because of a wish to avoid lengthy qualifications, this must be shown, and it cannot be shown simply by asserting (1).

No doubt there are differences between the feelings one has for fictions, at least sometimes, and those one has for real things, but none of these is itself enough to show that the feelings themselves are not the same in both cases. It is not uncommon to speak of different senses of words when the real differences have to do, not with the words, but with the things to which they are applied. Fear for the fate of Anna Karenina may seem different from fear for the fate of one's sister, but why deny that it is real fear? Fear of the dark is not the same as fear at the prospect of nuclear war. Fear that one has a serious illness is not the same as fear that one will be mugged on a dark street. Fear that one will be gored by a bull is not the same as fear that another person, the matador, will be gored by a bull. If my fear for Mrs. Mulwray in *Chinatown* is not as intense or long-lasting as my fear for my friend when he is serving in the army, and if it is not followed by grief as intense or long-lasting, well, perhaps that is just a difference between two things I may be in fear of.

Consider again the idea that if it were genuine fear, we would do something.

This, as it stands, is simply false: there are many cases in real life in which we encounter something fearful and do nothing because we can't do anything. Its being fictional is just one reason why we can't do anything.

And consider the idea that if the feeling were genuine, since the feeling would be unpleasant, if we could do nothing else, we would avoid the situation altogether.

As it stands, this is also false: in activities like automobile racing, mountain climbing, and bullfighting, both the participants and the spectators quite obviously experience genuine fear, and none of these people avoid the situation. In fact the presence of real fear is an integral part of the experience, and without it, there would be little interest in any of these enterprises.

The intuition that underlies the claim is the sense that we cannot have a genuine felt involvement, or any feelings or emotions, with regard to things whose existence we do not believe in. But perhaps the fact that we do have such feelings is exactly—and no more and no less—as surprising as the fact that we take any interest whatever in fictions. If one feels like saying "I couldn't have real feelings for nonexistent people," then why doesn't one, comparably, feel like saying "I couldn't take any interest in things that don't happen"? Here an assertion of Wittgenstein's seems exactly right. He says,

> Don't take it as a matter of course, but as a remarkable fact, that pictures and fictitious narratives give us pleasure, occupy our minds.[6]

He is right, this is a remarkable fact, and perhaps a fact that is in need of no special explanation, nor susceptible of any explanation, but a fact worth noting, a fact about human beings. It seems to me a natural extension from this fact about people that they take an interest in stories, to the intimately related fact that people's involvement in these stories includes genuine feelings.

The fact that I take an interest in the story of the movie *Chinatown* is interesting, and so is the fact that I fear for the fate of Mrs. Mulwray. If one finds either fact mysterious, one should be mystified by the other as well. I am willing to live with both mysteries, and I think it fruitless to attempt to *explain* either of them.

For an additional piece of what I suppose can pass for "evidence" in matters of this kind I offer what is probably an unexpected illustration. Although the topic is outré, and perhaps unseemly in the context of a sober text (or a text as sober as this one may be), it would be an oversight to omit the example of pornography. The question is whether we do, or even can have real feelings of the normal, pedestrian kind when the objects of

---

[6] *Philosophical Investigations*, Anscombe translation (New York: Macmillan, 1953), part I, paragraph 524.

such feelings are fictional, and, what's more, are known to be fictional, that is, known not really to exist.

Well, what of the feelings inspired by pornography, and, in particular, by the clearly fictional pornography to be found in stories and movies? It seems to me unmistakable and unarguable that the erotic feelings elicited by pornography in at least some people some of the time are exactly the feelings elicited in those readers and viewers by real people. No doubt it sometimes happens, in cases of deranged or deviate psychology, that someone is incapable of experiencing those feelings *except* in the case of fictional stimuli, and I suppose there are people who are never stimulated by fictional pornography. But there are many people whose erotic feelings are called up when they witness real events, when they participate in real events, and when they read or view pornographic fictions; and there seems to me no reason whatever to suppose that the feelings are not the same, and it also seems to me (admittedly an untutored observer of sexual psychology) entirely normal in these people.

I don't insist that my reasoning has been decisive, but it persuades me, and so I continue to speak as if the feelings aroused by fiction and other imaginary situations are exactly the same feelings as those aroused in real life, because that is what I believe them to be. To amplify the point, or at least to reinforce it, I add the following two examples.

It would be unaccountable if I paid no attention to what may be the most famous fictional passage dealing with this topic. The passage is a section of one of Hamlet's second-act speeches. Hamlet has just witnessed the First Player working himself into a lather as he recited lines describing the slaying of Priam and the effect of that killing upon Priam's wife. The Player has been greatly moved by the grief of Hecuba, and this surprises Hamlet who (memorably) asks, "What is Hecuba to him, or he to Hecuba?"

Hamlet is comparing the Player's response to the witnessing of a crime with his own response to learning of a crime, and he notes that while he himself is concerned with the crime of the murder of his father, the Player is concerned with someone's grief at the commission of a murder, and that someone (Hecuba) is not someone with whom the Player could have any direct connection. Hence the seeming embarrassment to Hamlet that he is less moved than the Player, when, seemingly, he has much more reason to be engaged.

But it is not merely that Hecuba means nothing to the Player. She is not simply someone outside the sphere of the Player's concerns. She is outside everyone's concerns, and we might ask, What is Hecuba to *anyone*? There was no Hecuba. She is a fiction. One might suppose this is of no concern to Shakespeare (or to Hamlet), but that supposition cannot be sustained, because in explaining his surprise Hamlet explicitly calls the Player's story "fiction," and Hamlet seems puzzled that anyone could be so moved by any mere story. [7] The phenomenon is even more enigmatic, as Hamlet sees it, because the fictional tale of Hecuba's horror and grief would seem, surely, less a stimulus to emotional arousal in anyone who hears or declaims it than the real-life stimuli to strong emotions present in Hamlet's (real) life, and yet Hamlet thinks he feels less strongly than does the Player.

Here we have layers upon layers to work through, and we would be as unlikely to pluck out the heart of the mystery of (the play) *Hamlet* as those who know him are to pluck out the mystery of (the character) Hamlet, even if there were far more space than I have here. I will mention only a few of the dimensions of this fabulously intricate matter, and do even that very briefly.

First is the fact that the Player is not the audience for the story, or not only that, but he is *performing* the story. (As Richard Strier puts it, we may have here an Elizabethan instance of "method acting.") But Hamlet immediately understands the

---

[7] Professor Richard Strier drew my attention to the striking use of this word, 'fiction', in Hamlet's speech, and he did that while helping me to understand many other things in the play. If the *Oxford English Dictionary*'s date line is correct and complete, the use of the word in this sense is found in the history of English not very long before Shakespeare's use of it in *Hamlet*.

potential for an audience, and surely it is this that encourages him in his design of some dramatic storytelling meant to have an effect upon his uncle/stepfather Claudius. And the stratagem works. When Claudius witnesses the wormwood assassination in the play, he is immediately and visibly aroused. Of course, for me, this is an example of Claudius's metaphorically identifying himself with the play's assassin, and then, for some reason, having feelings about his own act that, presumably, he did not have as a result simply of having done that act. Perhaps he is moved at least partly by the thought that his crime may be discovered, but I think it must also be true that his feelings are not simply those of a villain worried about being found out.

And now come the more obvious layers. If Hamlet can understand the possible emotional effects of a dramatic fiction, and make use of what he understands in order to work an effect upon Claudius, then how can it not be that Shakespeare, the maker of *Hamlet*, himself understands these possible effects and makes use of what he understands?

I find a striking affinity between Shakespeare's use of a play within a play in *Hamlet*, and Mozart's music within music in *Don Giovanni* (when the Don provides Leporello with the music of seduction). It is perhaps not only that method acting was known in the seventeenth century, but that modernism and postmodernism (so called and often waxed on about) are to be found in the seventeenth and eighteenth centuries.

In the book of Judges we read of the defeat and death of Sisera, general of the Canaanite army during the reign of King Jabin. You recall that at Deborah's urging, and with her by his side, the Israelite commander Barak engages Sisera's army in battle and defeats it. Sisera escapes and seeks refuge with Heber, thereby coming into the tent of Heber's wife Jael. After offering him refuge and a drink of milk, leading him to lower his guard and fall asleep, Jael kills Sisera. Afterwards, Deborah and Barak celebrate their victory in a song. This is a generally triumphal song, but its penultimate verse sounds a curiously compassionate note.

> Through the window peered Sisera's mother,
> Behind the lattice she cried:
> "Why is his chariot so long in coming?
> Why so late the clatter of his wheels?"[8]

    I suppose not all readers are touched by this passage, but those who are moved sense the worry and impending grief of a mother, a mother who is just beginning to dare to realize that the worst has befallen her child. One reader who was touched by these lines, and who heard in them reverberations of other dead children and bereaved mothers, is the poet Haim Gouri. Here is his poem (in translation from the Hebrew), "His Mother":

### His Mother

> It was years ago, at the end of Deborah's Song.
> I heard the silence of Sisera's chariot so long in coming.
> I watch Sisera's mother captured in the window,
> a woman with a silver streak in her hair.
>
> A spoil of multi-hued embroideries,
> two for the throat of each despoiler.
> This is what the maidens saw.
> That very hour he lay in the tent as one asleep.
> His hands quite empty.
> On his chin traces of milk, butter, blood.
> The silence was not broken by the horses and chariots.
> The maidens, too, fell silent one by one.
> My silence reached out to theirs.
> After a while sunset.
> After a while the afterglow is gone.
>
> Forty years the land knew peace. Forty years
> no horses galloped, no dead horsemen stared glassily.
> But her death came soon after her son's. [9]

---

[8] Judges 5:28.

[9] Collected in *Words in My Lovesick Blood*, poems by Haim Gouri translated and edited by Stanley F. Chyet (Detroit: Wayne State University Press, 1996).

Now consider how a reader feels about Sisera's mother, either a reader of Gouri's poem (who would, of course, already have to know the biblical story), or the original narration in the Bible. Readers of the Bible fall into three groups: those who read the text as an historical account that is generally factual, those who read the book as a fiction, and those who are agnostic about the veracity of the Bible's descriptions. My claim is that their feelings for Sisera's mother are the same, however they regard the text.

I don't insist that my reasoning has been decisive, but it persuades me, and so I continue to speak as if the feelings aroused by fiction and other imaginary situations are exactly the same feelings as those aroused in real life, because that is what I believe them to be.

I may well not have persuaded you, although I have persuaded myself, and if we thus differ, perhaps this is as much a difference in temperament as anything else. Sometimes what one philosopher finds obvious, a straightforward if remarkable fact, strikes another philosopher as being in need of an explanation. My temperament seems to resemble Mark Twain's. Responding to what he took to be a typically French, convoluted thesis, Twain wrote:

> It seems quite unlikely that that problem could have offered difficulties to any but a trained philosopher. [10]

Sometimes the most remarkable thing about a philosopher's temperament or sensibility is that he finds one thing in need of explanation but he thinks another, related thing is impervious to explanation. Hume thinks it is obvious that a person will act to increase his pleasure and decrease his pain, but he finds it mysterious that a person will act to affect the pleasure and pain of another person, and so he formulates his marvelously subtle

[10] Mark Twain, "What Paul Bourget Thinks of Us," first published in the *North American Review*, January, 1895; reprinted in *Mark Twain: Collected Tales, Sketches, Speeches, and Essays 1891-1910* (New York: The Library of America, 1992), where the quoted remark is on p. 175.

theory of *sympathy* precisely to explain this otherwise, as he sees it, enigmatic phenomenon.

If I haven't persuaded you that we have real feelings about fictions, at least I hope to have persuaded you that what you take to be a problem, the problem of our feelings for fictions, is no more or less a problem than that of the fact that we have an interest at all in stories. I will settle for that.

Whether or not I have persuaded you, I have no more to say about that topic, and I will close this chapter by introducing two related topics about which I have very little to say, but which I would like to interest you in.

The first is the question of our capacity for the unpleasant feelings aroused by some fiction. Here I would like to persuade you that the putatively problematic phenomenon of our engagement with stories, where that engagement is psychological, emotional, affective, and unpleasant, is not so very different from the phenomena of such engagements in real life.

The second topic, not quite so closely related, is the question of whether, and how, one might learn from fiction.

If I thought that our feelings about fictions were not our usual real feelings, then I would face no "problem of tragedy," because there would be no obviously unpleasant feelings whose pursuit needed explaining, but since I think the feelings are quite real, I have forfeited that way of avoiding the problem. Within the philosophy of art and literature, the question of unpleasant feelings tends to be called "the problem of tragedy," and the problem seems to be to find an explanation of why we submit ourselves to the undeniably unpleasant feelings induced, say, by *King Lear* or *Oedipus Rex* or *Chinatown*, or, for that matter, I suppose, by *And Quiet Flows the Don*. Most attempted explanations insist on a link of some kind between the unpleasant feelings and the other, pleasant feelings induced by those same works.

It will be good to have an example, and since we have already attended to bullfighting, instead of a standard tragedy let us consider García Lorca's familiar poem, "Lament for Ignacio Sanchez Mejias." You probably know this poem, and you know that it concerns a bullfighter dying of a mortal wound inflicted

by a bull's horn. Here is a part of the poem. It is the first of
four parts.

LAMENT FOR IGNACIO SANCHEZ MEJIAS

*1. Cogida and Death*

At five in the afternoon.
It was exactly five in the afternoon.
A boy brought the white sheet
*at five in the afternoon.*
A frail of lime ready prepared
*at five in the afternoon.*
The rest was death, and death alone
*at five in the afternoon.*

The wind carried away the cottonwool
*at five in the afternoon.*
And the oxide scattered crystal and nickel
*at five in the afternoon.*
Now the dove and the leopard wrestle
*at five in the afternoon.*
And a thigh with a desolate horn
*at five in the afternoon.*
The bass-string struck up
*at five in the afternoon.*
Arsenic bells and smoke
*at five in the afternoon.*
Groups of silence in the corners
*at five in the afternoon.*
And the bull alone with a high heart!
*At five in the afternoon.*
When the sweat of snow was coming
*at five in the afternoon,*
when the bull ring was covered in iodine
*at five in the afternoon*
death laid eggs in the wound
*at five in the afternoon.*
*At five in the afternoon.*
*Exactly at five o'clock in the afternoon.*

A coffin on wheels is his bed
*at five in the afternoon.*
Bones and flutes resound in his ears
*at five in the afternoon.*
Now the bull was bellowing through his forehead
*at five in the afternoon.*
The room was iridescent with agony
*at five in the afternoon.*
In the distance the gangrene now comes
*at five in the afternoon.*
Horn of the lily through green groins
*at five in the afternoon.*
The wounds were burning like suns
*at five in the afternoon,*
and the crowd was breaking the windows
*at five in the afternoon.*
At five in the afternoon.
Ah, that fatal five in the afternoon!
It was five by all the clocks!
It was five in the shade of the afternoon![11]

The poem was written about a real bullfighter and a real bull-fight, but it is often read as if it were fictional, and that is how I am treating it.

Many, many people have appreciated this poem, a work very effective even when translated out of its original Spanish. Per-haps it would do to say that many people have "liked" this poem. But surely they have also been disturbed and possibly even pained by the descriptions of the bullfighter's goring and subsequent lingering death. (Consider the lines "Death laid eggs in the wound," "In the distance the gangrene now comes," and "Horn of the lily through green groins.") Do these appreci-ators simply put up with that pain as a cost paid for the pleasure

---

[11] *The Selected Poems of Federico García*, edited by Francisco García Lorca and Donald M. Allen, with various translators (New York: New Directions, 1955), pp. 135–38. This poem is translated by Stephen Spender and J. L. Gili.

gained in reading or hearing the poem? Surely not, at least not if that means that they would, if they could, avoid the pain but retain the pleasure. Such a proposed trade-off makes no sense. It would be like trying to have the pleasure of drinking beer without actually drinking any beer.

Philosophers attempting to understand this seemingly enigmatic enterprise, the voluntary submission to the pain brought by art, have given many explanations, some simple and direct, some subtle and ingenious. Aristotle observes that some things found disagreeable in reality are pleasant when, as he puts it, they are "imitated." Hume believes that the intensity of the felt pain amplifies the pleasure given by beauty.

These philosophers may be right. I have no quarrel with them. Instead I have a suggestion, namely that the willing submission to pain as a part of human experience does not occur only with experiences of art, and that whatever remains enigmatic in our appreciation of artistic tragedy is equally enigmatic in our appreciation of some realities.

I turn again to bullfighting. Not quite a dozen years after the assassination of Lorca, the bullfighter Manolete, once a brilliant young prodigy, was sharing the ring with the young Dominguin, when he was gored and given a fatal wound in a bullring in Madrid. As you no doubt know, the event was particularly horrific and thrilling because Manolete was not gored by a bull passing by too close to miss the matador. In fact he was gored as he was killing the bull. He had plunged his sword deep into the bull when the bull, an especially fierce and unpredictable specimen, suddenly and unexpectedly swung his head sideways, impaling Manolete.

What of the audience at that bullring in Madrid in 1947? Surely they were pained by Manolete's goring, and then hurt more when they learned he had succumbed. Did they want Manolete to be gored? A preposterous suggestion. And yet I think it cannot be denied that bullfight spectators do indeed want there to be the possibility of death. This seems to me obviously to be the case, just as it is mentioned by one of today's premier mountain climbers, who said,

Without the possibility of death, adventure is not possible. [12]

So here, seemingly, is something of a paradox. Bullfighters, mountain climbers, automobile racers do indeed want, and need absolutely, the possibility of pain and death, but yet none of these adventurers (save for the deranged among them) wants any specific death to occur. And this is true of those who are spectators at events like bullfighting, automobile racing, and stunt flying. It can seem hard to understand, and harder to explain. There may be some simple or at least elegant analysis available, but I don't know it, and I will have to make do with this: the bullfight spectator both does and does not want the death of bullfighters. Surely no one in Madrid that day wanted Manolete killed by the bull, and, I would guess, neither Lorca nor anyone reading his great poem wants Ignacio killed. And yet, as the mountain climber says, without the possibility of death, bullfights would not be what they are, and bullfight spectators want bullfights to be what they are, and so they want the possibility of death. Perhaps this is not a paradox but a kind of *omega*-incompleteness. Suppose I am a bullfight lover. I do not want Manolete to die, I do not want Ignacio to die, I do not want Dominguin to die, and so on and on; but I think it cannot be true that I do not want *anyone* to die, for what can it be for death to be a possibility if there is never death?

Is this an enigma awaiting a solution, or is it just one more *fact* about human beings and what they do? I have no answer to that question. What I have is the thought that whatever this is, it is the same as the so-called problem of tragedy. The case of pain from art may be special in any number of ways, but it is, still, one instance of a way that humans behave in real life. In all these cases there is the oddity that I both want and do not want something. Earlier I said that when reading *And Quiet Flows the Don* I did not want Pyotr to be executed, and I think that is true. But it is also true that I found it good that Pyotr was shot, and in that regard I wanted it to happen, because

---

[12] Reinhold Messner, often called the world's greatest mountaineer, quoted in *National Geographic*, November 2006, p. 44.

Pyotr's death is important to a long theme of the novel, the eventual outcome of Grigory's life in which he has participated in a war he neither wanted nor understood, and after that war he is utterly bereft, now without his wife, without the other woman—the one he loved best, and without his only brother.

So there is a difference. Those who watched Manolete die did not want him to die even though they did want the death of bullfighters because they wanted the possibility of death, while those who read the Lorca poem both do and do not want Ignacio to die.

There are other differences between the embrace of pain in fiction and the embrace of pain in real life, and in the case of bullfighting, for instance, although the events and consequences are real, the affair is, so to speak, separated from quotidian life, is, so to speak, *framed*, but I will leave it for another time and for other philosophers to examine those differences. I will move to the other topic, that of the question of learning from fiction.

In a cavalier remark near the end of chapter 3, the chapter about Nathan and David, I said that stories can instruct, and that sometimes they are meant to instruct. It is far from obvious that this is true, and so I will take a moment here to make the point that it is true, that one can learn from stories.

All I can do here, and it might be all I could do anywhere, is to establish the fact that we can and do learn from fiction, and I would like to do this simply and incontrovertibly despite the murky clouds looming over most grandiose claims and counterclaims concerning "truth in fiction." I do this by turning to a splendid example, an example almost certainly familiar to you, but likely to be unexpected in this context. It comes from J. L. Austin's essay "A Plea for Excuses," and it is in the section in which Austin helps us begin to understand the varied ways in which we excuse, explain, justify, and otherwise account for our pieces of untoward behavior. Here is what he says:

> As practice in learning to handle this bogey, in learning the essential *rubrics*, we could scarcely hope for a more promising exercise than the study of excuses. Here, surely, is just the sort of situation

where people will say 'almost anything', because they are so flurried, or so anxious to get off. 'It was a mistake', 'It was an accident'—how readily these can *appear* indifferent, and even be used together. Yet, a story or two, and everybody will not merely agree that they are completely different, but even discover for himself what the difference is and what each means.

And then Austin appends this footnote:

> You have a donkey, so have I, and they graze in the same field. The day comes when I conceive a dislike for mine. I go to shoot it, draw a bead on it, fire: the brute falls in its tracks. I inspect the victim, and find to my horror that it is *your* donkey. I appear on your doorstep with the remains and say—what? 'I say, old sport, I'm awfully, sorry, *&c.*, I've shot your donkey *by accident*'? Or '*by mistake*'? Then again, I go to shoot my donkey as before, draw a bead on it, fire—but as I do so, the beasts move, and to my horror yours falls. Again the scene on the doorstep—what do I say? 'By mistake'? Or 'by accident'? [13]

Examples like this are common in philosophy, especially in analytic philosophy, although virtually no one was as good at giving them as Austin, and he never gave a better one than this donkey example. But common or not, what are they? Austin calls them "stories," and surely this is what they are, and they are fictional stories at that. How could it be otherwise? Austin is addressing the reader directly, using the second-person pronoun 'you', and I must be that person when I am reading "A Plea for Excuses." Well, I don't own a donkey, and have never owned a donkey. I don't know whether Austin ever had one, but I am, as the positivists would say, "morally certain" that he didn't, on two occasions, assassinate a donkey, both times getting the wrong one.

Of course this is not a story like Joyce's "The Dead" or Flannery O'Connor's "Everything That Rises Must Converge" or Doyle's "The Speckled Band." But it is a story, or two stories,

[13] J. L. Austin, "A Plea for Excuses," in J. L. Austin, *Philosophical Papers* (Oxford: Oxford University Press, 1961), p. 132, with accompanying fn. 1, p. 133.

or a story in two parts; and it is, unquestionably, fiction. And, unquestionably, it *teaches* something. It teaches us, or reminds us, of the difference between doing something by mistake and doing something by accident. Now it may very well be, as any number of philosophers and others have opined, that those masterpieces by Joyce and O'Connor teach, and maybe so does the delightful Sherlock Holmes story, but intriguing as those pedagogies may be, they are also problematic, and I will not enter the debate over whether they do, in fact, genuinely teach anything, or even *say* anything. I will stay with Austin's parable, for there, it seems to me, there is no doubt whatever that it teaches. Nor will I take up other examples from the long history in philosophy of the use of storytelling examples. That history includes Plato's story of the ring of Gyges, Nietzsche's fabricated tale of Zoroaster, and, of course, much of the philosophy we know in the form of dialogue, including, perhaps preeminently, Hume's magnificent *Dialogues Concerning Natural Religion*.

The Austin example is enough for my purposes, which are modest but determined. Whether or not fictional stories take us into some other "world," a fictional world, they can teach us about our world, the real world, and they also can inspire real-world feelings.

# CHAPTER FIVE

## *More from the Bible: Abraham and God*

That man was not a learned exegete, he didn't know Hebrew,
if he had known Hebrew, he perhaps would easily have
understood the story and Abraham.
—SØREN KIERKEGAARD[1]

A MORE forbidding passage of biblical narration is in the book
of Genesis, where Abraham is told by God to sacrifice his
son Isaac. You recall that Abraham sets about complying with
God's directive, and he proceeds right to the point at which he
would kill Isaac, and at that point God sends an angel to call
Abraham off.

This is a story of great difficulty. To grasp the story—or at
least to try, to try to begin grasping it—it seems to me necessary
to try to appreciate Abraham, and that means asking what it
would be like to be Abraham.

Compare Abraham's near-sacrifice of his son Isaac with Agamemnon's sacrifice of his daughter Iphigenia. The proposition
comes to Agamemnon in the context of a choice. Sacrifice Iphigenia and the winds will blow, the fleet will sail, and the Greeks
will prevail over Troy. Refuse to sacrifice her and none of that
will happen. To this Agamemnon adds (perhaps hopefully, only
to exculpate himself) that if he refuses to make the sacrifice, the

---

[1] *Fear and Trembling*, "Prelude"; *Fear and Trembling and The Sickness unto
Death*, translated by Walter Lowrie (Princeton: Princeton University Press,
1941), p. 27.

Greeks will be enraged and will set upon him and his household. Thus Agamemnon's choice, however painful and monstrous, is compelling—as a choice.

Abraham has no such choice. He is already committed, for he has previously made a contract with God that obligates him to do this thing God now asks. Immediately after Isaac's escape, Abraham shows himself a master of contracts when he secures a burial site for his wife Sarah, and in the course of this transaction he instructs others in the matter of contracts.

I find it easier to imagine being Agamemnon than to think of myself as Abraham. Agamemnon and his predicament, however alien, seem more familiar to me than Abraham and his trial.

Can you imagine what it would be like to be spoken to by God? Can you imagine believing God is speaking to you?

I have heard it said, "I would not kill my son even if God told me to do it," or "I would not believe it was God asking me to kill my son."

My first thought is yes, I too wouldn't believe it was God asking, and if I did, I wouldn't do what He asked. But then I think—what would it be like—really—to believe God was speaking to me? [2]

Of course it is very, very difficult to imagine being willing to kill one's child. It is terrifying and numbing even to attempt this imagination. But however difficult it is to imagine this, or to imagine doing many of the other things Abraham does, these imaginings are predicated upon a prior act of imagination, namely, imagining yourself in conversation with God. I do not think I can do that. Can you?

---

[2] In the *Euthybro*, Socrates, presumably speaking for Plato, says that it is not the approval of the gods that makes things holy, but, rather, that the gods approve of things *because* they are holy, implying that there must be some other test of holiness. Kant agrees, insisting that even the acts of Jesus are to be tested against the categorical imperative (presumably passing the test with flying colors). It is when one believes this, obviously, that one supposes anyone claiming instructions from God where those instructions lead to a putatively immoral act has not in fact heard from *God*. It is possible to disagree with this, as both Dostoevsky and Wittgenstein do, each of them taking the word of God to have absolute precedence. I take no stand on this question, at least not here. My

Suppose you undertook to sacrifice your child, believing God to have told you to do this. I tell you not to do it, maybe even try to stop you. If I told you I was an angel of God, or a representative Thereof, and maybe believed it myself, would you believe me? Do you know how to go about answering this question?

---

only concern is with the case in which one is dealing with someone who *does* think that the approval of God itself overrides any other consideration.

# CHAPTER SIX

## *More Lessons from Sports*

The fans sitting up there are *helpless*. They can't pick
up a bat and come down and do something. Their only
involvement is in how well you do. If you strike out or mess
up out there, they feel they've done something wrong.
—WILLIE McCOVEY[1]

[Bernard King] will never get up to the level of the
real all-timers like, say, Kareem, or myself, because he
looks like he's working too hard. When you reach a
level of greatness there's a certain added element that
goes into making it look easy.
—JULIUS ERVING[2]

IF THERE is something to be learned about fellow feeling from
considering the lot of the sports fan, there is yet more to learn
from sports—two things, at least. One is the question of just
how virtuosity is appreciated, and the other is the question of
that sense of personal involvement known to the ardent fan.
The questions are related.

In working through this chapter I have been helped considerably by conversation with and comments from three exceptionally acute fans, Shoshannah
Cohen, Elmer Almachar, and Amos Cohen.

[1] Quoted by Roger Angell, *Late Innings* (New York: Random House, 1982),
p. 105.

[2] Quoted by Mark Jacobson in "Doctor One and Only," *Esquire*, February,
1985, p. 116.

Virtuosity might be thought to be the exhibition of something difficult done without apparent effort. If that is so, then the appreciation of virtuosity requires an awareness of the difficulty of the accomplishment, and if the difficult has been made to look easy, as Julius Erving says sometimes happens, then how is it that the audience knows that it is not as it looks, that it is truly difficult? There are only two possible answers, I think. The first answer is that the audience might just be familiar with statistics or other data concerning the act in question. One might just know that those trying to do something, say, lay down a good bunt during a suicide squeeze, or hit behind the runner on a hit-and-run play, or pass a basketball accurately with either hand, do not often succeed. From this one could infer that it is difficult to do these things. I think that is true, but it is, so to speak, to apprehend the difficulty from the outside, by indirection. On the other hand, one might have personal acquaintance with The relevant attempts, either in fact or in one's imagination. Can you *feel* yourself attempting to bunt a baseball several feet up the third base line when the pitcher has thrown you a 95-mile-per-hour fastball, aiming it in the vicinity of your head? If so, then you certainly know that this is one very difficult thing to do because you can, in imagination, feel how difficult it is.

Questions of difficulty and virtuosity arise not only in the appreciation of sports, of course, but also in the appreciation of art. In certain sports, for instance diving and ice skating, the estimate of a performer's attempt includes a reference to the difficulty of what was attempted, and in this way it is possible to think that something's difficulty is actually part of the thing being done, although it is not always easy to hold on to this idea. The idea has been expressed by the great pianist Claudio Arrau, who said this:

> Take the beginning of the Beethoven Opus 111. People play it with two hands because they don't want to risk dirty octaves. Well, first of all, it sounds different played with one hand, as written. And then technical difficulty has itself an expressive value.
>
> The way it's [Brahms's F-sharp Minor Sonata] written is almost impossible—to make the big skips fortissimo. Actually, *without*

*exception* people redistribute the notes. Here, for instance, they take the bottom notes in the right hand—F-sharp, C-sharp, A, F-sharp—with the left hand. . . . And then, of course, it's very easy. Again, I must say that such facilitation is wrong. Physical difficulty has itself an expressive value. When something sounds easy, its meaning changes completely.[3]

I have no doubt that Arrau is correct—speaking for himself. But what of the rest of us, and especially what of those who do not play the piano, and even more urgently, what of those who do not play the piano or have much familiarity with piano-playing? Arrau is a consummate pianist, and as such he may, as he says, *hear* the difficulty in what is being played. I'm not sure the rest of us can do that. Not only are we unlikely to be able to hear the difficulty, we may not even be aware that what we are hearing *is* difficult. On this point, at least, a comparison between musical virtuosity and virtuosity in sports seems apt. In both cases, something difficult is being done, and the full appreciation of that achievement must require an awareness of the difficulty, and there is the question of how the audience comes to be aware of that. In both cases, unless an audience member is aware of what might be thought of as the over-all probability of the thing's being done, what it needs is the ability to imagine doing the thing and therein to encounter its difficulty.

A tangential question suggests itself here, and it seems worth noting, although it will be left hanging because it has no bearing on the topics of this book. The question, in both sports and art, is, when is a difficult thing worth doing? When is it laudable to do a difficult thing? Not every difficulty is worth overcoming. For instance, it is, unquestionably, very difficult to play the piano with such force that the instrument breaks (as Liszt is reported to have done). It is also difficult, in basketball, to drib-ble the ball with one finger instead of one's whole hand. But in neither case is this difficult doing going to count as a laudable

---

[3] Quoted in Joseph Horowitz, *Conversations with Arrau* (New York: Knopf, 1982), pp. 121, 152–53.

virtuosity. It must be that the difficulty-mastering must somehow be integral to the general achievement of which it is a part,
and it is not at all easy to explain this. It is, thus, not easy to
explain the logic of one of Aristotle's arguments for the preeminent importance of plot in tragedy. Aristotle gives a number of
arguments for this conclusion, the final one being the observation that beginning tragedians achieve success in constructing
plots later than they achieve success in creating other parts of
a tragedy. This sounds like a claim that it is relatively more
difficult to construct a plot, and Aristotle links this to his assertion that it is a more valuable or important thing to do. Fortu-
nately for us, we need not, here, concern ourselves with this.
What does concern us is a little more thought about the condition of the kind of audience members who are fans.

A fan hopes his team will win, but not all who hope for a win
are fans. And there are some who are fans but are not *complete*
fans, not purely fans.

Someone who bets on a team to win then hopes it wins because he will then win something, how much depending upon
the size of his wager, the odds, *&c.* This spectator's interest in
the outcome of the game is, so to speak, mediated by an interest
that attaches him to the outcome, and thus he is not, so to speak,
directly linked to the team and its fortunes.

There is also the kind of fan who attaches himself to a team
exactly because he expects the team to win, and as it becomes
clearer that his team is unlikely to win, he ceases to be engaged.
Such a spectator, typically, is called a 'fair-weather fan'. This
appellation is negative, certainly, and it seems to carry a tone
of moral disapproval, as if this fan is not sufficiently loyal or
committed.

A fair-weather fan is like a fair-weather friend; in fact such a
fan may be a kind of fair-weather friend. [4] It is perhaps obvious
that a fan is a kind of friend to the team or competitor of which
he is a fan, and if he is only a fair-weather fan, then, just like a
fair-weather friend, he deserts the team when things go badly:

---

[4] As nice a point as this may be, it had not occurred to me until David Hills
pointed it out.

he ceases to take an interest and may even become indifferent to the team's fortunes. It is less obvious, I think, that a fan is something of a friend to other fans of the same team. He joins them in their pleasures and pains as their team succeeds and fails. If he is a fair-weather fan, then it is not only the team he deserts in bad times, but also his formerly fellow fans, and thus it is not only the team that will find him faithless, but also the true fans, those whose attachment to the team remains whatever the team's success.

Surely it is possible to *choose* to be a fan of some team, but a surprisingly large percentage of fans do not explain their attachments in this way. They say, rather, for instance, that their parents were already fans, and it is with their parents that they first became at all interested in watching, say, baseball, and, somehow, watching with a parent already a fan, they turned into fans. This is how I became a fan of the Chicago White Sox, and it is worth noting that although my father is now long dead, it does not seem to me an open possibility that I should cease to be a White Sox fan. Others seem to have had their condition as fans thrust upon them by the accidents of where they live, or what team's games they could receive on radios or television sets, and, of course, some seem to become fans "automatically" by attaching themselves to the teams of the colleges they attend.

An interesting phenomenon, not at all uncommon, is that of the fan *against* a team or an individual competitor. This partisan is, so to speak, a negative fan, an anti-fan. Whether or not there is a particular team this fan is a fan *of*, he is definitely opposed to some particular team. Thus he is not one of those who in the first instance are hoping that a particular team win; rather, he is hoping that a particular team lose, and he may well thus be hoping that any team playing against that team will win. I tend to hope that the Minnesota Twins and Cleveland Indians baseball teams lose, but only because they play in the same division as my White Sox and their losses contribute to the Sox's chances of winning their division. When, as may happen late in the season, either of them falls out of contention, I no longer care that they lose. With the New York Yankees, however, things are different. Their fortunes during the regular season are unlikely to have much bearing on the White Sox's chances of getting to postseason play (unless the wild card is in question); and yet I wish for them to lose almost every time they play, the only exceptions being when, in interdivisional play, they play against the Twins or the Indians (and even then, my feelings are mixed).

Some anti-fans are as keen, even rabid, in their negative hopes, as regular fans are in their hopes for positive outcomes. There is a little of the anti-fan in me, though not nearly of the strength of my wish for the White Sox to win. I do, at least a little, or maybe more than that, wish for the Yankees to lose. My passions are much less excited by football, but there, too, some of them are negative, and I do, often, wish for the Fighting Irish of Notre Dame to lose.

There is a peculiar case in which the positive and negative aspects of fan life are linked, and this is to be found in cities with more than one team, and, sometimes, in states with more than one team or university. In Chicago, for instance, where there are two baseball teams, the White Sox and the Cubs, many partisans of either team are devoted to the failure of the other team, even though these teams virtually never compete against one another, and their few head-to-head meetings are seldom of much overall significance.

It is important to distinguish cases like the ones just mentioned from ones involving intense rivalries but only derivative negative wishes. In North Carolina, for instance, there is, annually, a strong, highly partisan basketball rivalry between the University of North Carolina and Duke. And there are such rivalries in baseball, a sport I know much better—for instance, between the New York Yankees and the Boston Red Sox, and between the Chicago Cubs and the St. Louis Cardinals. In these cases, however, the anti sentiment is, more or less, simply the concomitant of the positive sentiment. A fan of the University of North Carolina basketball team will indeed be hoping for a Duke loss *when* Duke is playing against UNC, but, in my experience, such fans do not usually care very much how Duke does when it is playing anyone else. Cub fans may "hate" the Cardinals, but it doesn't seem to matter much to them whether the Cardinals win or lose when they are not playing the Cubs. In fact, a devoted Cubs fan may well be hoping that the Cardinals do well enough to advance to the playoffs, where they can be beaten by the Cubs.

As in the rest of life, these allegiances and enmities can be complicated. An example is found in a group I belong to. During the baseball season, a number of us exchange email messages almost daily, offering comments, condolences, complaints, and inspiration as the fortunes of the White Sox wax and wane. The group includes my son Amos, my daughter Shoshannah, and her husband Elmer. All of us are White Sox fans. A close friend of my son's, however, Robert Hochman, is a Yankees fan. It is not decent to hold this against him because he comes by his condition honestly, being from New York, although he now lives in Chicago. Occasionally there are three-way correspondences between my son, his friend, and me, and then I find myself in the interestingly difficult position of hoping the Yankees lose, especially when they are playing the White Sox, but being unable to take any pleasure whatever in the pain this may cause Hochman. He is a very decent man, and, at the end of the 2005 season, he even congratulated us on the White Sox World Series win, and, indeed, said he had supported the White Sox as soon as the Yankees had dropped from contention. I have, somehow, to incorporate at least a little empathetic pain from Hochman's team's loss, although my dominant feeling is of pleasure at his team's loss, and I can do that. It is no more difficult than what is required of us in living the non-sporting parts of life with other people, and it is no less difficult than that.

# CHAPTER SEVEN

## *Oneself Seen by Others*

O wad some Power the giftie gie us
To see oursels as ithers see us!
—ROBERT BURNS[1]

A VITAL exercise, perhaps too seldom undertaken, is the effort
to appreciate how one may be appreciated by others. Think of
someone significant in your life—a friend, your spouse, your
lover, a student of yours, or a teacher. Now ask yourself, how
do you strike that person?

This is a marvelously intricate task, very difficult to do because it requires, so to speak, both leaving yourself and bringing
yourself along. First you must imagine yourself to be the other
person, and then, in your newly-imagined embodiment, you
must look back at the real you and discover what you see. Are
you an ardent student, or a sycophant; an inspiring teacher, or
a tiresome pedant; a considerate and skillful lover, or at best as
a competent and repetitive mechanic?

Those of us who write are sometimes bewildered and sometimes angered by those who write reviews of what we write. I
have written something very deep; he finds it trite. I have said
all that can be said; he finds my writing incomplete and unfin-
ished. When I read these responses I say of the reviewer, he is
a poor reader—careless and too quick—or he is biased, or he is

[1] *To a Louse.*

stupid. [2] But when I have calmed, I might ask, how is it that my writing can have struck him in this way? I might try to imagine him reading my work. This can be chastening and instructive, even if he *is* stupid and a sloppy reader.

The ways in which one person understands another has been given an exceptional literary illustration in A. B. Yehoshua's novel *Mr. Mani*. [3] In each of the five "conversations" that make up the book, one reads an extended conversation between two people, but learns only what one of them has said, leaving one's grasp of the unheard person coming solely from his effect upon the other. In each case $A$ is speaking to $B$, and we never learn what $B$ has said. From what $A$ says we infer, first, something of $A$'s character, but then, also, something of $B$'s character so far as we can make that out from what $A$ says to him or her.

---

[2] One might wish to make use of the appraisal offered by a character in a novel who refers to "the review of your new book by the dumbest, clumsiest, shallowest, most thick-witted, wrongheaded, tone-deaf, tin-eared, insensate, and cliché-recycling book-reviewing dolt in the business." (Said by one of the characters named 'Philip Roth' in Philip Roth, *Operation Shylock* [New York: Random House, 1993], p. 314.)

[3] Translated from the Hebrew by Hillel Halkin (New York: Doubleday, 1992).

# CHAPTER EIGHT

## Oneself as Oneself

*Az ikh vel zayn vi er, ver vet zayn vi ikh?*
*[If I should be someone else, who would be me?]*
—Yiddish saying

THERE IS a special example of metaphorical personal identification, peculiar, perhaps, but common, in which the person one identifies with is oneself. This happens when one tries to gain a sense of oneself at a future time. It is at the center of the hypothetical thinking one engages in when making current decisions that will have future effects.

Suppose I am asked to be nominated to run for the office of president, say, of the American Society for Aesthetics or of my division of the American Philosophical Association, and I must decide whether to accept the nomination. I begin by imagining how I would feel if I won the election, and how I would feel if I lost. Others would no doubt approach the question with more equanimity, but given my insecurity and the quirks of my personality, I find the question difficult. I think, if I lose the election, I will be disappointed, of course, and, being who and what I am, I may try to mitigate my disappointment by supposing that my loss is the product of a benighted electorate, a group of stodgy and unimaginative academics incapable of appreciating my work. Such a supposition might soothe me. But having entertained this supposition in advance, what will I feel like if I win the election? Won't I have depreciated the contest to a point at which I could take no pride in being the choice of electors I was prepared, if only provisionally, to denigrate?

In contemplating the possible outcomes in preparation for deciding whether to stand for election, it seems to me that I imagine myself in the future, both as winner and loser of the election. This is not imagining myself to be another person, not exactly, but it is similar to that, for it is imagining myself in future circumstances. It is imagining myself to be me-in-the-future, and that person, a future me, is not the current me.

The imagination of oneself in the future is one of the most common of our contemplations. It is the background and prelude to countless decisions ranging from a decision about what career to pursue to the choice of what to have for dinner.

I regard this act of imagination, too, as the grasping of a metaphor. Identifying oneself with another person is a special case of metaphorical identification, and identifying oneself with oneself-differently-situated is, thus, a special special case.

# CHAPTER NINE

## *Lessons from Art*

We also say of some people that they are transparent
to us. It is, however, important as regards this observation
that one human being can be a complete enigma to another.
We learn this when we come into a strange country with
entirely strange traditions; and, what is more, even given a
mastery of the country's language. We do not *understand* the
people. . . . We cannot find ourselves in them.
—LUDWIG WITTGENSTEIN[1]

THE PHENOMENON of mutual human understanding is itself frequently a theme within narrative art. When this happens, the
reader, as must be his custom, busily at work discovering the
extent to which he can imagine being the various characters
in the text, is also presented with something of a meditation
upon the extent to which anyone, ever, can achieve this kind of
understanding. An excellent example, perhaps the preeminent
example, is the work of Joseph Conrad, especially in his *Heart
of Darkness*. But before turning to that bleak text, I will say
something about a very significant work that seems to me to
have *Heart of Darkness* as its progenitor. Curiously, it too is by
a Polish artist.

[1] *Philosophical Investigations* (New York: Macmillan, 1953), part II, p. 223.
This is the Elizabeth Anscombe translation slightly altered by me. Anscombe
translates "Wir können uns nicht in sie finden" as "We cannot find our feet
with them." I have not read the line as an idiom, and have translated it as "We
cannot find ourselves in them."

A central theme in Roman Polanski's movie *Chinatown* is the inability of the character Jake Gittes (played by Jack Nicholson) to understand another character, Noah Cross (John Houston). When Gittes has become aware that Cross has done terrible things—theft, conspiracy, incest, reckless homicide, outright first-degree murder—he asks Cross why he has done these things, and he expresses his own puzzlement by listing reasons why he imagines anyone would have done them, and tells Cross that they do not seem to apply to Cross. What Gittes is doing is imagining what reasons *he* might have that would lead him to do these things, and although such reasons might have force for Gittes, he cannot see how they could move Cross, and thus Gittes cannot understand Cross, cannot grasp why Cross has done what he has done. Cross answers that he has done them "for the future," and this answer makes no sense to Gittes.

Noah Cross is a monster, whose monstrosity is evident in his utter lack of interest in how things look and feel to anyone else, and this shows in his refusal to learn and acknowledge even the name of the Nicholson character. Despite being corrected, he persists in calling him, not Gittes, but Gitts.

Gittes has been warned by Mrs. Mulwray (Faye Dunaway) that he will be unable to understand Cross, but in his arrogance he has refused to believe her. Perhaps the triumphal assumption that we can easily understand one another is as sinful as the refusal to attempt any human understanding at all, and that would mean that our obligation is to try grasping one another in the full realization that it cannot be done with complete success.

I believe that what Polanski calls 'Chinatown' is what Conrad calls 'the heart of darkness'. The two works share the theme of the limits of human understanding, of the existence in our world of things and people we cannot decipher. [2] The novel has a more complex narrative structure, however, and you will

---

[2] A poignant meditation on this theme is Richard Stern's story "The Illegibility of This World," first published in *Commentary*, February, 1992, and included in his anthology *From Almonds to Zhoof: Collected Stories* (Chicago: Triquarterly, 2005).

forgive me for reminding you of what "happens" in *Heart of Darkness*, and forgive me again for doing it crudely.

*Heart of Darkness* is narrated in the first person, and the narrator at the beginning of the book, the end of the book, and intermittently in between is an unnamed man, referred to only by the pronoun 'I'. Almost all of the book, however, is narrated by a man named Marlow, whose narration is quoted by the I-narrator. From Marlow's narration we learn the following.

A young Belgian man named Kurtz makes a journey to a place in Africa, where he is to be the representative of a Belgian trading company. Marlow makes a journey to that place in order to retrieve Kurtz. Kurtz speaks to Marlow about what has happened to Kurtz since his arrival in Africa, although we are told almost nothing of what Kurtz tells Marlow. Marlow speaks of all this, including his having been spoken to by Kurtz, to a group of friends some time later, a group including the first-person narrator of the book. That narrator speaks (or writes) of all this to whoever reads the book.

That is a clumsy retelling. I will add a little more, just as clumsily. Soon after being found by Marlow, Kurtz dies; he dies on Marlow's boat while Marlow is carrying Kurtz away, back down the river. A year or so later Marlow dies a kind of moral death, when, back in Brussels, he lies to Kurtz's fiancée about how Kurtz died and what Kurtz said when dying. The I-narrator does not seem to die in any way, and yet is profoundly changed, on his ship, as he listens to Marlow tell his story of Kurtz's telling his story. And then, finally, there is the reader, seeking to "identify" with the narrator, the narrator who, in his earlier turn, has identified with Marlow, Marlow who yet earlier identified with Kurtz.

Is all this identifying really possible? Sometimes, at least, it seems impossible. Wittgenstein registered this opinion when he wrote the remark used as an epigraph for this chapter.

Wittgenstein is a real person talking about real people, in real life. A stronger and gloomier observation is voiced in *Heart of Darkness* when Conrad's narrator Marlow, evidently losing confidence that his hearers can understand him, interrupts his narration to exclaim,

> . . . No, it is impossible; it is impossible to convey the life-sensation of any given epoch of one's existence—that which makes its truth, its meaning—its subtle and penetrating essence. It is impossible. We live, as we dream—alone . . .[3]

Is it hopeless, then, to fathom another human being? Perhaps not. Wittgenstein began by noting that in fact we seem to find some people transparent, and Conrad's narrator Marlow is not entirely pessimistic, for he goes on to say,

> Of course in this you fellows see more than I could then. You see me, whom you know . . .

So if we already knew someone, he might be able to let us understand something of him, his feelings, his actions, his life. And how would he do this? Conrad's narrator does it by telling a story, and telling it to people who know him. But Conrad himself is telling the story in which this story is told, and Conrad cannot expect us readers to know him—except through this story. Can this succeed?

I think this ability to tell stories that promise to secure human understanding is nothing more or less than one of the powers of art. And I think our ability to be reached by this power is itself nothing more or less than what we could call our moral imagination, and that, I think, is deployed in our comprehension of what I am calling metaphors of personal identification.

When I presented an early version of some of this work, at the University of Minnesota, it was pointed out to me by professors Marcia Eaton and Naomi Scheman that I was being too sanguine about the propriety of these acts of imagination in which one may achieve a measure of sympathy with another. As they noted, in some cases this may well lead to a failure of moral judgment as one comes to feel "at one" with someone who is highly immoral, perhaps even a moral monster. Thus if I bend my imagination to understanding Hitler, say, or Stalin,

---

[3] There are many extant editions of *Heart of Darkness*, many of them reliable, and I have thought it less helpful to cite one of them than to point out that this passage occurs about a third of the way through the book.

or Mao, I may begin to feel a kind of "rightness" in doing what they did and then be unable to appreciate how wrong it was to do those things. Eaton and Scheman are right, surely, and notice must be taken of this.

There has lately been a resurgence of interest in the question of possible connections between aesthetics and ethics, or, a little more specifically, of the relation of art to morality. I am myself persuaded that there is a superabundance of evidence showing that a refined appreciation of art does not lead to any discernible improvement in the morality of such appreciators. And yet there is a connection, as I see it, between the ability to fully appreciate narrative fiction and the ability to participate in the morality of life, precisely because the ability to imagine oneself to be someone else is a prerequisite for both. It does not follow that one's moral participation will be improved, however, because the questions remain open, first, of what one reads, and then of what one will do once one has appreciated another person. To indulge in the jargon of analytic philosophy, one might say that imagination is a necessary condition for a competent moral life, but it is not sufficient.

In a remark as striking in its insight as in its blindness, Virginia Woolf observed this:

> The reason why it is easy to kill another person must be that one's imagination is too sluggish to conceive what his life means to him.[4]

Surely this is right as an explanation of the ease with which some can kill, but it fails utterly to recognize that it may be exactly one's ability to imagine the cost to another that makes it possible to wish to kill him.

In fiction, just as in life, one may find a character opaque, or transparent, or something in between, and one's capacity to *reach* the character is likely to be variable.

---

[4] Quoted from Woolf's diary by Curtis Sittenfeld in his review of *Virginia Woolf: An Inner Life* by Julia Briggs, *New York Review of Books*, November 20, 2005.

When *A* undertakes to imagine being *B*, his chance of success is not to be understood as somehow abstractly objective, because it will depend critically upon just who *A* is. When *A* imagines himself to be *B*, he will be obliged to meld his own characteristics with those of *B*, and, of course, this attempt will encounter impossibilities when some of the former characteristics are inconsistent with some of the latter. Is there some *essence* of *A*, something that makes him uniquely *A*? This is a debatable question, and it need not detain us, for whether or not any of *A*'s characteristics are essential, there are bound to be some characteristics, essential or not, that will not fit with characteristics of *B*. *A* is either unable or unwilling, in imagination, to abandon those features of himself that will have to go if he is truly to imagine being *B*. Whether *A* does possess such incompatible characteristics (incompatible with those of *B*, that is) depends upon who *A* is, and thus for some *A*'s it will be possible to imagine being *B*, while for other *A*'s it will not. I think this may be how it is in cases like my own attempts to engage Edith Wharton's characters. Here I encounter difficulties stemming from the physical characteristics of the characters, although these are not great and insuperable difficulties, and also difficulties in thinking of myself as acting as the characters do, as well as holding their beliefs and attitudes.

In the plot of Wharton's *House of Mirth*, the destitute heroine Lily Bart seems to have a chance at a kind of survival if she marries her Jewish acquaintance Simon Rosedale. [5] During the course of the story she declines his proposal, and later he declines hers. She is thus consigned to a miserable fate, although perhaps she or Wharton think it a nobler end than being married to Rosedale. Throughout the novel we find a number of remarks about Rosedale, including these half dozen:

> He was a plump rosy man of the blond Jewish type, with smart
> London clothes fitting him like upholstery, and small sidelong

---

[5] My thinking about my relation to this novel has been stimulated and, I hope, improved by conversations with Shoshannah Cohen, who knows the book far better than I.

eyes which gave him the air of appraising people as if they were bric-a-brac.

He had his race's accuracy in the appraisal of value, and to be seen walking down the platform at the crowded afternoon hour in the company of Miss Lily Bart would have been money in his pocket, as he might himself have phrased it.

. . . Rosedale, with that mixture of artistic sensibility and business astuteness which characterizes his race . . .

He knew he should have to go slowly, and the instincts of his race fitted him to suffer rebuffs and put up with delays.

. . . a little flushed with his unhoped-for success, and disciplined by the tradition of his blood to accept what was conceded, without undue haste to press for more.

"If you'd only let me, I'd set you up over them all—I'd put you where you could wipe your feet on 'em!" he declared; and it touched her oddly to see that his new passion had not altered his old standard of values.[6]

The text is not entirely clear as to exactly whose views these are, Lily's or the author's. I read the book as if the opinion were held by both Lily and the author, but this makes no difference because I wish only to ask the question, how am I to identify, either with the author or with Lily Bart, or, for that matter, with Simon Rosedale, when that identification seems to require assuming a certain opinion of Rosedale specifically, and of Jews in general. I am myself a Jew, although not of the plump, rosy, blond type. Of course I am a latter-day Jew, unlike the Jewish character of Wharton's novel, and, possibly, quite unlike the American and European Jews of Wharton's world. I have some artistic sensibility, I suppose, but not much business astuteness; I have some patience, but I am not inclined to suffer rebuffs.

[6] Edith Wharton, *House of Mirth* (New York: Charles Scribner's Sons, 1969), pp. 14, 15, 16, 121, 178, and 300. For those consulting other editions, it should help to know that the first five quotations come from book 1, chapters 1, 2, 2, 11, and 15, respectively, and the last is from book 2, chapter 11.

Can I, in imagination, connect myself with this description and conception of Jews? Must I then imagine myself to hold certain opinions I believe to be false? Must I, for instance, believe Rosedale to have certain traits that Lily correctly believes him to have, or do I suppose Rosedale not to have those characteristics but Lily (and perhaps Edith Wharton) truly to believe he has? Can I imagine myself *being* a Jew of whom this opinion would be accurate? And could I suppose that, in fact, virtually all Jews including me have such traits?

As I have been saying, I believe I think of myself as another in order (1) to discover how things look to another, and then (2) to sense how things feel when seen in that way. I seem to reach limiting cases when, even in imagination, I cannot exchange my characteristics for those of the other I'm trying to imagine myself to be, or even blend my characteristics with his.

Here are two very long-standing ideas about art, neither of them very clear and both of them irresistible. The first is at least as old as Aristotle. It is the idea that at least some works of narrative art are somehow both universal and absolutely, specifically particular. It is absolutely, specifically the story of Oedipus Rex or King Lear or King David or Roy Hobbs, and yet, somehow, it is not only about that. The second idea is at least as old as romanticism. It is the idea that at least some works of art teach me something about myself, or allow me to discover something about myself. Together the two ideas suggest that the story of Roy Hobbs is a story about me. I love this suggestion, and I would love it more if I could make it clearer. The best I can do is to suggest that my full *appreciation* of the work requires of me that I grasp the metaphorical identification in which I see myself to be Roy Hobbs. Perhaps I cannot achieve a full appreciation of *House of Mirth* just because I cannot see myself as I would if I were Lily Bart or Edith Wharton. It is then an open question whether the deficiency is mine, or Edith Wharton's. And then, again, there may be no deficiency at all, just the fact of the differences between people, some differences being unnegotiable.

I do a little better with Henry James than I do with Edith
Wharton, but not much. Someone who cares even less for
James than I do is V. S. Naipaul, who has said this:

> You only have to look at that dreadful American man Henry
> James. The worst writer in the world actually. He never went out
> in the world. Yes, he came to Europe and he "did" and lived the
> writer's life. He never risked anything. He never exposed himself
> to anything. He travelled always as a gentleman. When he wrote
> English Hours about what he was seeing in England—written for
> an American magazine—this man would write about the races at
> Epsom and do it all from a distance. He never thought he should
> mingle with the crowd and find out what they were there for, or
> how they behaved. He did it all from the top of a carriage or the
> top of a coach. A lot of his writing is like that. And he exalts his
> material because he thinks that this subject matter he has alighted
> on—the grandeur of Europe and the grandeur of American new
> money—is unbeatable. Elizabeth Hardwick said to me about
> Henry James many years ago, "What's he going on about? These
> people he is talking about are just Americans!" It has the effect
> that young American people still think they can "do a Henry
> James"—come to Europe and write a book like Henry James.[7]

There must be more than a little history and psychology at
work in these successful and failed imaginings, and my problem
with James is not the one Naipaul has.

I am able to imagine myself to be one of William Golding's
primitive characters, or someone with the opinion of scientific
farming held by Levin in *Anna Karenina*, or someone with de-
fective medical views like the father in Turgenev's *Fathers and
Sons*, despite those characters' holding beliefs and engaging in
actions inconsistent with my own beliefs and actions. My difficulty in doing this with Wharton's characters may be due to
my conviction that, unlike those benighted views held by the
characters of Golding, Tolstoy, and Turgenev, views which have

[7] Published as "V S Naipaul talks to Farrukh Dhondy," in *Literary Review*,
April, 2006.

largely disappeared from my world and are, in any case, of no threat to me, the view of Jews held by Bart/Wharton seems to me still alive in my world and very much a threat to me. Someone who did not feel threatened, whether he were a Jew or not, then might very well succeed where I fail, and indeed fully imagine the characters of *House of Mirth*.

With Henry James, however, my estrangement is different. Unlike Naipaul, I have no difficulty with James writing as an American, or with his failure (if indeed it is that) to present any characters from the English "crowd" or any non-would-be-aristocratic Americans. My problem is that I am nearly unable to *care* for James's characters. I don't seem able to grasp the remarkableness of Isabel Archer, and thus I don't find my way inside the characters who do find her remarkable, and I cannot even gain much sense of James's own conception of her allegedly remarkable being.

I do not defend Naipaul's distance from James, nor do I defend my own. If you would like to blame either of us, assigning us a shortcoming, then I don't mind. I ask only that you accept the truly remarkable fact that this variability in readers' appreciation and understanding of fictional characters is no different from the variability we display when we come to like, love, dislike, hate, empathize with, blame, and praise the real people who inhabit our real world.

# CHAPTER TEN

## *The Possibility of Conversation, Moral and Otherwise*[*]

> Moreover, political education is not merely a matter
> of coming to understand a tradition, it is learning
> how to participate in a conversation.
> —MICHAEL OAKESHOTT[1]

IT MAY happen in moral discourse and also in seemingly less
weighty conversation that I find myself frustrated and say of my
adversary, "I just don't understand him."[2] The other party has
failed to come round to my view. Sometimes 'I don't understand him' is a way of saying that he is the one who has not
*understood* something. Perhaps he has not grasped my point,
or my reasons; and perhaps he has failed at this because he is
inattentive or dense or stupid, or perhaps he simply hasn't tried.
But if he has followed my every step, has understood everything
I've said, and still hasn't come to share my view, then when I
say I don't understand him, just what do I mean? I think I mean

---

* Perhaps there is no "otherwise."

[1] "Political Education," a lecture delivered at the London School of Eco-
nomics in 1951, printed in *The Voice of Liberal Learning: Michael Oakeshott on
Education*, edited by Timothy Fuller (New Haven and London: Yale University
Press, 1989).

[2] I doubt that the official moral conversations so often considered in moral
theory are in fact any more significant than human conversation in general.

exactly what I say—*I do not understand him*. And this remark is
at least as much about me as about him.

Think of a person as the sum of his beliefs, feelings, and
actions. Then unless he has the same beliefs, feelings, and actions as I, he and I are not the same person. It is this fact that
leads me to say that he does not understand me when the other
person does not agree with me. But surely this is asking too
much. The wish to agree with one another in all things might
be thought of as a wish that we could live together speaking
exactly the same language. Then that futile wish is the failed
ambition to build the Tower of Babel. And the biblical lesson,
in part, is that God does not want us to agree in all things.

So just *what* don't I understand? What is it about him that
outruns my understanding? It is this: he knows what I know,
sees what I see, hears what I hear, and yet he does not feel (or
act) as I do. How can he be like me in the rest, but not in this?
And the answer, of course, is that he can be very like me but
not entirely, exactly because he is not me.

When this gulf is met, what are you to do? And what is he
to do?—After all, he does not understand you either.

What is wanted, I think, is an *appreciation* of one another.[3]
This is the form understanding will take if it is to bridge
this gulf.

It is critical to understand that appreciation is not agreement.
I do not turn myself into you: I do not become you. The proposition that I am you is not a literal identification. It is a metaphor. It must be possible for me to understand you, and in that
sense to accept you, without agreeing with you. If it is not possible, then we are doomed.

It is possible, at the last stage, that there is nothing attractive
to appreciate. There is nothing there besides ignorance, stupid-

---

[3] What I am calling "appreciation" is, I think, related to what Stanley Cavell
has called "acknowledgment." (Stanley Cavell, "Knowing and Acknowledg-
ing," in his *Must We Mean What We Say?* [New York: Charles Scribner's Sons,
1969]. The book was republished [Cambridge: Cambridge University Press,
1976].) The word 'appreciate' suits my purposes because it suggests the connection between doing justice to another person and responding adequately to
works of art.

ity, or delusion. We cannot—should not—always give in. When confronting mystics, spiritualists, or vulgar Freudians, the impasse may leave you unable to *credit* the other person. You may be unable to decide even whether he is sincere. But if you accept his sincerity, then he believes ingenuously that he is in touch with some other world, that he communicates with the surviving spirits of the dead, that he knows the true motives of people (perhaps including you) better than they do themselves. You don't believe he knows and does these things, although you have no doubt that he is sincere. What then?

Even then it is good to identify the exact deficiency, and, perhaps, even to imagine what it is like to be afflicted with it. It is especially useful to do this when there seems to be the possibility of *fraud*. In my work I find this question arising with works of art, with some criticism of art, and—in philosophy and nearby—certain expositions of "theory." I find a work of art to be of no merit, or at best of very little substance. I find a piece of art criticism to be ungrounded. I find some literary theory, cast in terms of excruciating difficulty, to be at best mostly vacuous and partly banal, and at worst mostly meaningless and partly false. What do I think of the artist, critic, or theorist?

Now I would not myself make such art or write such words. What do I discover when I imagine myself doing so? If I imagine myself still thinking of these things as I do, then I may imagine myself as a fraud. That is, I would be a fraud if I found these words or art meaningless, false, banal, or incomprehensible, and yet still set them out as *mine*. And I would be not only a fraud but a corrupter if I set them out with the hope that others would be taken in, would believe them to be significant while I believe them to be empty.

But if he *does* believe these things he says, does find meaning in them, then he is not a fraud in any simple sense, and it will not be so easy for me to take his measure.

The topic of fraudulence is wide and difficult, and it is not a central topic of this book, but it may be useful to think about it a little.

Suppose some person $A$ is involved with some object $X$ (a phrase, perhaps, or a text, or a joke), and either $A$ doesn't believe *X*, or *A* doesn't know the meaning of *X*, or *A* doesn't find *X* funny, and yet *A* presents *X* to *B*.

Suppose there is a correct, standard, natural relation *A* might have to *X*. Then if *A* hopes to induce *B* to believe that *A* stands in this relation, *A* is engaged in some kind of fraudulence (the kind depending upon just what the thing in question is). But if *A* has no such hope, and wants no such result, and may even declare that he himself doesn't believe, or understand, or laugh, then he may just be giving *X* to *B*, and there is no fraud. And if then *B* does find himself in the proper relation to the thing, this might just have been a nice gift, even if there is a fracture in the transaction.

For instance, I don't care for Brooks Brothers clothing. I don't wear it myself, and I don't much care to see it worn by others. But I know you like it. I give you some. That's OK, and maybe even better. It is an attempted *appreciation* of you by me—especially if I not only predict that you will like to have it, but can imagine liking to have it. I imagine being you.

Another kind of disconnection, similar but also quite different, occurs when one recites prayers or sings songs in languages one does not oneself understand, or when one tells a joke without comprehending it. A speaker may undertake such enterprises because of what, in some sense, he thinks they "mean" and what results he hopes to achieve, but he cannot do these things, so to speak, from the inside. He is not a fraud, but neither is he altogether whole.

Intelligence has little to do with the capacity for metaphorical personal understanding, at least intelligence as it is typically, narrowly construed. Indeed there are forms of intelligence that seem to work against interpersonal understanding. There is a kind of intelligence especially likely to be found in universities, in my experience, very ready to assign stupidity or some other disability to those who are different. Both inside and outside the academy is to be found a kind of pseudo-intelligence in the form of one of those ideologies that includes, built-in, an explanation of those one does not understand. This explanation, in fact, is either a pretense to understand or a refusal to admit that there is anything to be understood. In possession of

one of these "systems of thought," one says of one's opponent, "He is repressing," "He is trapped in his ideology,"
"His class consciousness blinds him," "He is an infidel," "He
is possessed," "He is hysterical." These "analyses" or "diagno-
ses" are, typically, nothing more than the speaker's oblique con-
fession of his own ignorance about the person he presumes to
be explaining.

A classical impasse in mutual understanding occurs between
a religious person and an adamant skeptic, or between two differently religious people, when each has a "diagnosis" of the
other. The skeptic supposes his opponent to be "superstitious,"
probably as a result of childhood experiences. The believer
thinks the skeptic is untouched by grace, somehow not even a
"disciple at second hand." This stalemate is dramatized brilliantly by Hume in his *Dialogues Concerning Natural Religion*,
when one of his characters, Cleanthes, says,

> Consider, anatomize the eye; survey its structure and contrivance,
> and tell me, from your own feeling, if the idea of a contriver
> does not immediately flow in upon you with a force like that of
> sensation. [4]

To this, some will answer 'Yes' and some 'No', with everyone
speaking the truth. I think Hume knew that, and that those
readers who suppose that Hume was simply giving an argument
in favor of one opinion over two others have failed to understand why Hume chose to write a *dialogue*. In a dialogue, at least
in one as brilliantly written as Hume's, there are real characters
presented, and, as always, the reader may identify with one or
more of them. If you can identify with Cleanthes and also with
the other characters, then you will find yourself, alternately,
giving in to Cleanthes' remark, and resisting it. You will then
appreciate that some will say 'Yes' to Cleanthes, and some will
say 'No'. Then what will they do?

[4] Hume, *Dialogues Concerning Natural Religion*, part III.

# CHAPTER ELEVEN

## Conclusion: In Praise of Metaphor

[Metaphor] is the great human revolution, at least
on a par with the invention of the wheel.
—YEHUDA AMICHAI[1]

So THERE they are, these metaphors of personal identification.
They are the entrées to human understanding, to the appreciation of one another. They demand to be grasped. Grasping
them is part of one's commitment to being human, for being
human requires knowing what it is to be human, and that requires the intimate recognition of other human beings. This is
certainly not a new idea, and it has never been put more clearly
than by a man of the theater:

> I regard the theater as a serious business, one that makes or should
> make man more human, which is to say, less alone.[2]

It may seem desirable that there be a "method" for grasping
these metaphors. One would employ a formula, or a procedure,
or at least a routine. But there is none, no more than there
can be a functional formula for delivering the import of any
interesting metaphor, or of any significant work of art.

[1] Quoted by Mel Gussow in his obituary notice for Amichai, *New York Times*,
September 22, 2000.
[2] Arthur Miller, *Arthur Miller's Collected Plays* (New York: The Viking Press,
1957), p. 11.

The metaphors, the art, the people would all be dispensable if their measure could be taken by a formula. There are no formulas for this, thank God.

In that remark of Yehuda Amichai we have hyperbole, no doubt, but Amichai was not only a very good poet but also a very serious thinker, and if I am nearly right about the need for metaphor in the enterprise of being human, then perhaps Amichai is right, and it is difficult to overestimate the importance of our capacity for metaphorical understanding.

So there they are—the metaphors and the art, including the metaphors that can connect you with others. The metaphors, the art, and the people demand that you grasp them. And you can do this only by investing your self.

# Index

Aaron, 25
American Philosophical Association, 67
American Society for Aesthetics, 67
Abraham, 53–54
Absalom, 25n.6
Agamemnon, 53–54
allegory, 9–10, 9n.7
Almachar, Elmer, 57, 63
Alter, Robert, 19
Amichai, Yehuda, 85–86
Amnon, 25n.6
analogy, 9
*And Quiet Flows the Don*, 33–36, 48–49
Aristotle, 30, 47, 60
Arrau, Claudio, 58–59
Austin, J. L., 49–51

Bart, Lily, 74–76
Beethoven, 58
Black, Max, 24
Bledstein, Adrien J., 27n.7
Brahms, 58
Bruns, Gerald L., 9n.7
bullfighting, 30–31, 44–48
Burns, Robert, 65

Cavell, Stanley, 80n.3
Chicago Cubs, 31, 62

Chicago White Sox, 31, 61–63
*Chinatown*, 31, 37–38, 70
Churchill, Winston, 5–6
Cohen, Amos, 57, 63
Cohen, Shoshannah, 57, 63, 74n.5
Conrad, Joseph, 69–72
Cross, Noah, 70

David, 11, 19–27, 49, 76
Deborah, 41
*Dialogues Concerning Natural Religion*, 51, 83
*Doctor Faustus*, 32–33
Dominguin, 47
*Don Giovanni*, 41
Dostoevsky, 54n.2
Doyle, Arthur Conan, 50–51
Dunaway, Faye, 30, 70

Eaton, Marcia, 72–73
Erving, Julius, 57
*Exodus*, 25

fans, 60–63

Gittes, Jake, 70
God, 30, 53–55
Goodman, Nelson 24
Gouri, Haim, 42

*Hamlet*, 39–41
Hass, Robert, 10
*Heart of Darkness*, 69–72
Hills, David, 60n.4
Hobbs, Roy, 76
Hochman, Robert, 63
*House of Mirth*, 74–78
Houston, John, 70
Hume, David, 47, 51, 81

Iphigenia, 53
Isaac, 53
Isenberg, Arnold, 6, 22–23

Jabbar, Kareem Abdul, 57
James, Henry, 77–78
*Jeremiah*, 25
Jews, 74–76
Joab, 19, 20, 25n.6
Joyce, James, 50–51
*Judges*, 41

Kant, Immanuel, 30, 54n.2
Kierkegaard, Søren, 53
King Lear, 76
King, Bernard, 57
Kurtz, 71

Lorca, Garcia, 44

Mann, Thomas, 32–33
Manolete, 47–48
Marlow, 71–72
McCovey, Willie, 57
Messner, Reinhold, 48
metaphor, *passim*, esp. 1–11, 16–17,
    68, 80, 82, 85–86
Miller, Arthur, 85
Moore, Marianne, 29
Moses, 25
Mozart, 41
*Mr. Mani*, 66
Mrs. Mulwray, 30, 37–38, 70
Mussolini, Benito, 5–6

Naipaul, V. S., 77–78
Nathan, 19–27, 49
New York Yankees, 61–63
Nicholson, Jack, 70
Nietzsche, 51

Oakeshott, Michael, 79
O'Connor, Flannery, 50–51
Oedipus Rex, 76
*Oxford English Dictionary*, 13,
    40n.7

parable, 9
Pinsky, Robert, 19
Plato, 51, 54n.2
Polanski, Roman, 30, 70
pornography, 38–39
Proulx, E. Annie, 29

Rosedale, Simon, 74–76
Roth, Philip, 66n2
Russo, Richard, 29

*Samuel*, 19–27
Saul, 25
Scheman, Naomi, 72–73
Shakespeare, 40–41
Sholokhov, Mikhail, 33–36
simile, 2–3, 9–10
Sisera, 41–43
Solomon, 25
*Song of Songs*, 10
sports, 13–17, 57–63
Stern, Josef, 1, 1n.3
Stern, Richard, 3–5, 4n.5,
    70n.2
stories, 19–27, 29–51, 69–78
*Story of a Novel*, 32–33
*Straight Man*, 29
Strier, Richard, 40, 40n.7

Tamar, 27n.7
Twain, Mark, 43

University of Minnesota, 72
University of Notre Dame, 62

Wharton, Edith, 74–78
White, Roger, 1, 1n3.

Wittgenstein, Ludwig, 38,
 54n.2, 69
Woolf, Virginia, 73

Yehoshua, A. B., 66